Year-Round Education
A Collection of Articles

Edited by
Robin Fogarty

IRI/Skylight Training and Publishing, Inc.
Arlington Heights, Illinois

Year-Round Education: A Collection of Articles

Published by IRI/Skylight Training and Publishing, Inc.
2626 S. Clearbrook Dr.
Arlington Heights, IL 60005
800-348-4474 or 847-290-6600
Fax 847-290-6609
info@iriskylight.com
http://www.iriskylight.com

Creative Director: Robin Fogarty
Managing Editor: Julia Noblitt
Editors: Amy Wolgemuth, Sabine Vorkoeper
Proofreader: Troy Slocum
Type Compositor: Donna Ramirez, Christina Georgi
Formatter: Donna Ramirez
Illustration and Cover Designer: David Stockman
Book Designers: Michael Melasi, Bruce Leckie
Production Supervisor: Bob Crump

ISBN 1-57517-020-5
LCCN: 97-73109

1735-4-98 V
Item number 1388
06 05 04 03 02 01 00 99 98   15 14 13 12 11 10 9 8 7 6 5 4 3 2

Contents

Year-Round Education
A Collection of Articles

Education today, more than ever before, must see clearly the dual objectives: education for living and educating for making a living.—James Mason Wood

Have you heard about schools looking into or moving toward block scheduling, regrouping students into "families" or "houses," rearranging youngsters into multiage clusters, forming and facilitating teacher teams, designing school days and calendars to incorporate chunks of time for professional development, or appointing study groups to examine the concept of year-round education? If you haven't, you probably aren't living in North America. For there is a current sweeping across this continent, one that is bringing radical structural change to schooling as we know it.

As schools embrace curricular reform that involves what is sometimes referred to as "chunked curriculum"—problem-based learning, thematic instruction, project-oriented experiences—those on the front lines are finding it necessary to reevaluate traditional, almost sacredly held beliefs about how schools are structured. Under intense scrutiny are student grouping policies, in response to research that has surfaced about tracking; daily timetables and schedules, because of the emphasis on integrated, authentic, and relevant learning that is not only brain compatible, but also brain enhancing; and, last but not least, school calendars, because communities are responding to current indicators suggesting that continuous schooling benefits many sectors of society.

From the demands of working moms and latchkey children to school boards' insistence on fiscal responsibility, from the psychological factors that support continuous, uninterrupted learning models to the politicians' view that more time in the classroom means higher standings for our youth in the international arena, the call for year-round education is once again being heard. This collection of pertinent articles has been assembled to inform a public dedicated to the best schooling a nation can offer. Each article has been selected for its timeliness, its particular perspective, and its inherent value in presenting a balanced view of the many faces and facets of this intriguing and complex issue.

The articles are arranged in three distinct sections: Year-Round Education: General Information; Year-Round Education: Examples at Work; and Year-Round Education: The Change Process. The five articles in the first section focus on the general information one needs in order to make an informed decision about year-round schooling. Included in this initial grouping are discussions outlining the historical context of the movement, a rationale that offers solid justification for making the shift to year-round schools, how services are impacted and the cost factors involved, as well as a comprehensive look at the pros and cons of this innovation.

The second set of essays presents authentic examples of year-round schools, ranging from a K–8 elementary school and an at-risk elementary school to a high school and an over-crowded K–12 school. The final article showcases a college that has adopted the year-round framework. Each article presents a distinct vision of year-round schooling. Together, the spectrum of models offers fertile ground for insightful discussions, reflective thought, and viable comparisons, both for individual consumption and for various public forums.

In the final section, composed of five articles, the focus is on the change process that carries the idea of year-round education from conceptualization to implementation. One of the articles demystifies the traditional nine-month school; another presents the argument that year-round schooling can reduce costs and improve student achievement. In yet another piece, public opinion is sampled as a component of the change process, while one other essay suggests that the year-round school acts as a magnet that attracts many elements of school reform. A final discussion outlines seven rules that guide the change to year-round education.

Year-Round Education: General Information

Every man has a right to his opinion, but no man has a right to be wrong in his facts.—Bernard M. Baruch

Y ear-round education (YRE) is, perhaps, an idea whose time has come. While the movement has a long and varied history, the current focus seems to be rooted in the academic benefits rather than in the cost-effectiveness of overcrowded schools. In fact, the rationale is rich with testimonials about why year-round education is under scrutiny as a viable alternative as schools search for ways to expand students' "time to learn."

As an investigation into YRE begins, stakeholders often need an introductory look at the "big picture." They want to quickly gather facts about the history, the rationale, the benefits and barriers, and the change process involved. This first section, entitled "General Information," is designed to do just that—to give a quick overview of YRE as a backdrop for further study.

Citing a 1991 federal analysis of "time and learning," Anderson delineates possible options for time and learning that include extended day, extended year, year-round, and reorganized day. Referred to as "promising practices," the options are explored more fully with descriptions of actual schools trying them. Supported by well-researched facts, this essay offers insight into the academic rationale for YRS.

In a piece about "the basics," Glines presents a succinct yet comprehensive discussion that speaks to the history, the methods, the concerns, and the future of year-round education. Taking the reader back to the early 1900s, the author spotlights early attempts at year-round schooling and then brings in specific information on current trends.

The author states that, while increasing enrollment is the driving force behind the current mini-explosion of year-round schools, year-round education is also advocated for its other benefits. Some schools even offer families a choice between a nine-month or a twelve-month calendar, in hopes of creating a "win/win" environment for all involved. In addition, Glines summarizes various calendar plans, highlighting the many options available once communities begin to reevaluate their current school calendar. This enlightening article ends with a brief listing of the pros and cons surrounding the issue of year-round education and predicts its continued expansion in the years ahead.

A second article by Glines presents the philosophical rationale for year-round education, organizing the reasons into three areas—societal needs, personal factors, and space concerns. Then, the author describes how communities usually approach the idea of year-round education. In the concluding discussion, the author offers an appealing analysis of the rationale by delineating eight reasons for moving toward year-round education—continuous learning, employment realities, lifestyle diversities, curriculum facilities, improvement catalysts, community enhancements, people considerations, and personal choices. Each of the aforementioned ideas seems to provide material for further investigation for communities interested in the concept of year-round education.

To cap off the argument, Glines underscores, in an emphatic comment, a theme threaded throughout the article: "It does not make sense for community learning centers to stand empty for three months. Parents do not close hospitals (also helping institutions) for the same period." While his bias is evident, the article is well worth reading to examine the many plausible arguments for year-round education.

Exemplified by the statement "School facilities are one of the most underutilized components in the educational organization," the article by Bradford offers a comprehensive cost analysis of the impact of year-round education. The author addresses the issues of support services, transportation, operation, facilities, and maintenance, concluding with useful information on break-even points for schools moving toward year-round schooling. His closing argument—that allowing hotel rooms, hospital rooms, and classrooms to remain vacant for long periods is not an efficient, effective way to use such facilities—underscores an earlier allusion that effective results noted in promotion, remediation, enrichment, and acceleration can be achieved through YRS, also.

Concluding this first section on general information about year-round education is an essay by Mutchler that stresses the two major concerns addressed by year-round schools—efficient use of facilities and maximizing student learning outcomes. The discussion also summarizes mechanisms for local implementation, including pilot schools, schools-within-a-school, plan-within-a-plan, and paired and clustered schools. In addition, the benefits and difficulties of implementation are highlighted, and policy considerations, fiscal impact, and changes in student achievement are discussed thoroughly, with fairly positive conclusions.

Alternative Approaches to Organizing the School Day and Year

A National Commission Examines New Structures for Improving Student Learning

by Julia Anderson

In the last decade, our nation has watched young people from other countries outpace our own in scholastic achievement. At the same time, business and industry have cited our students' lack of academic skills to keep our nation technologically and economically competitive.

While the current commitment to improving the U.S. educational system is to be applauded, true and lasting change will not occur unless and until we address time and learning issues. Time as an educational variable has yet to capture the attention of school reformers.

In its landmark 1983 report, *A Nation at Risk,* the National Education Commission on Excellence in Education urged America's schools to allocate "significantly more time" to learning: "This will require more effective use of the existing school day, a longer school day, or a lengthened school year." Of all the recommendations made in *A Nation at Risk,* the commission's suggestion regarding the use of time probably has received the least attention.

> True and lasting change will not occur unless and until we address time and learning issues.

From *The School Administrator,* vol. 51, no. 3, March 1994, pp. 8–11, 15.

Attention to time issues has increased with the establishment of the national goals and the concomitant effort to establish curriculum frameworks, new assessments, and standards for all students. These developments in education have combined with changes in the social demographics of the United States to place new demands on schools. In the 1990s, most women work outside the home and 82 percent of the women in the work-force have school-aged children. In addition, the number of single-parent families has risen to 14.9 million and the number of at-risk students is expected to grow by more than one-third in the next few decades.

> Schools have the capacity to refine— and even redefine— their role.

Using time as the lens, or prism, through which to view education reform, several schools have responded to the increased demands by experimenting with reorganizing time. These experiments offer a fresh perspective on creative time use in schools to increase student learning.

By varying the ways in which time is used for learning, schools have the capacity to refine—and even redefine—their role, shaping themselves to meet the goals of the education reform movement and the needs of a changing population.

FEDERAL ANALYSIS

Since 1991, the National Education Commission on Time and Learning has been examining the quality and the adequacy of the time U.S. students devote to learning. The commission has studied:

- length of the school day and year;
- how time is used for learning academic subjects;
- use of incentives to increase student achievement within available instructional time.
- how children spend their time outside school, including time spent on homework;
- year-round professional opportunities for teachers;
- how states might change rules to facilitate a longer day and year;
- analysis and estimate of costs; and
- use of school facilities for extended learning programs.

What follows is not intended to suggest the commission has reached its final conclusions (which will be issued in a report in April), nor does it necessarily represent the views of commission members. Rather, it constitutes a personal reflection on information heard in the course of our work.

At the time the commission began its work in April 1992, we identified only 10 schools with "extended learning programs" that offered 210 days or more of schooling. Since then, a number of other schools and districts have been experimenting with innovative time arrangements, indicating, perhaps, the beginning of a trend.

In an effort to adapt to new expectations, schools throughout the nation are developing and implementing alternative models of school time. The commission has visited a number of these sites.

POSSIBLE OPTIONS
During the last year, the commission also has listened to the views of a broad range of practitioners, researchers, policy makers, representatives from business, parents, and students regarding time and learning. We also have received testimony from acknowledged luminaries in education.

Through public hearings we have reached out to communities across the country for innovative ideas. This consultation process has allowed us to identify many schools that provide creative time use at the grassroots level. Some models demonstrate imaginative uses of existing time allocations, while others are based on providing extended time—a longer school day, a longer school year, or both.

Innovative programs of time use address one or more of the following concerns:

• provision of additional learning opportunities for enrichment or remediation;

• parents' interest in their children's well-being;

• business interest in having employees focus their attention on productivity rather than worrying about the safety of their children;

• efficient use of school facilities and other resources; and

• use of the school building as a locus for services by community agencies.

DEFINING TIME

Alternative time uses can take various forms—extended day, extended year, year-round, and reorganized day or week. Many schools, of course, offer a combination of alternative time uses.

Schools with an extended year program also may offer an extended day or a reorganized day to provide additional learning opportunities for children, including remediation and enrichment. Some school districts have adopted a shortened week (four days), another type of alternative time use.

Some of the innovations based on time allocations include these:

• *Extended Day:* A longer school day and/or before- and after-school programs; usually includes a traditional academic day (e.g., 8:30 a.m. to 3 p.m.) with extended time for learning opportunities and support services for social needs.

• *Extended Year:* School years in excess of 200 days for various reasons, including those cited above.

• *Year-round:* Schools that redistribute the 180 days, allowing for shortened summer breaks and several breaks during the school year; schools are categorized as single-track or multi-track. (Multi-track means students attend on a rotating basis because the school cannot accommodate all students at one time.)

• *Reorganized Day:* Varying the length of the learning experience based on student need or curriculum demands, i.e., block scheduling.

PROMISING PRACTICES

The following alternative models of school time are illustrative; neither the list of models nor the list of schools is comprehensive. The purpose here is to provide information on such practices to stimulate schools and communities around the country to undertake their own experiments in allocating time for improved learning.

Selected as representative examples are the Murfreesboro, Tenn., district, extended day; the Beacon schools in Oakland, Calif., extended year; Emerson Elementary School in Albuquerque, N.M., year-round; and Piscataquis Community High School in Guilford, Maine, reorganized day.

EXTENDED DAY

The Murfreesboro City Schools run an extended day program on a year-round basis. The program operates from 6 a.m. to 6 p.m. (Three schools are open an additional three hours for adult learning). The academic day is from 8 a.m. to 3 p.m. The district serves more than 4,000 children in eight elementary schools; more than half participate in the Extended School Program.

The Extended School Program provides academic learning experiences, skill-building, exploration, experimentation, and problem-solving. It also provides increased learning time for those students who require remediation. All students, moreover, receive individual attention from trained adults and child care at a minimal cost to parents (maximum $26 a week). Only families that use the service pay for it.

> **Students receive up to four hours and 45 minutes of additional learning time a day.**

Students receive up to four hours and 45 minutes of additional learning time a day during the regular school year, and they can participate in a rewarding summer program.

The Murfreesboro program represents a highly efficient use of costly school facilities by providing additional learning time for elementary students as well as adult learners. Interested adults can take computer training courses as well as basic reading, math and GED courses during the hours of the extended program.

Murfreesboro finances the program through a combination of parent fees, creative staffing, and Chapter 1 funds.

The program started in January 1986. (Contact Becci Bookner, Murfreesboro City Schools, Extended School Program, Box 279, Murfreesboro, Tenn. 37133-0279, 615-893-2313).

EXTENDED YEAR

The Beacon Day School and Beacon High School in Oakland, Calif., operate for $10^{1}/_{2}$ hours a day, from 7:30 a.m. to 6 p.m. The academic day is from 8:30 a.m. to 3 p.m. The elementary school is open 240 days a year; the high school provides 215.

Beacon can be categorized as extended year, extended day, and reorganized day.

Beacon schools are private, non-denominational, ethnically, and economically diverse, and designed around the concepts of developmental education and year-round education.

Both schools offer a 12-month program in which students, grouped in multi-age, multi-skilled ability groups rather than by age or grade, progress at their own rates. Each class has at most a 24-month chronological span. Children remain in a given class until they have mastered the skills necessary to move on to the next level.

> Children remain in a given class until they have mastered the skills necessary to move on.

Mastery is demonstrated through regular classroom work; formal testing rarely is used, letter grades never are used at the elementary level, and classes are cooperative and non-competitive. No homework is assigned until the ninth grade. Because so much time is spent on task, individual study habits are developed during the day.

The curriculum includes four major components: core skills; integrated studies; advisory; and experiential studies. Teachers are trained in developmental education methods and participate in site-based management through a teacher council. The faculty teaches for 210 days a year but is paid for 260 days. Teachers on a rotating vacation schedule are covered by eight permanent, full-time substitutes (called flex teachers).

No set vacation is established. Instead, families plan vacations to meet their own schedules. Students returning from vacation simply pick up where they left off since the school provides individualized instruction.

Approximately 95 percent of the parents participate in volunteer activities at the Beacon schools and the schools offer classes on parenting and child development. Tuition is $490 a month for elementary and $575 for high school, comparable to per-pupil costs of the Oakland Public Schools.

Fifteen percent of the student body receives financial aid. The schools are funded by tuition from parents and by corporate and private contributions.

The program began at the day school in September 1982 and at the high school in September 1991.

(Contact: Leslie Medine, Beacon Day School and Beacon High School, 2101 Livingston St., Oakland, Calif. 94606, 510-436-6462)

YEAR-ROUND

Emerson Elementary School in Albuquerque, N.M., operates on a 12-week-on, 15-day-off, multitrack schedule. The cycle occurs three times a year. The entire Albuquerque school district is on vacation for three weeks in July.

During the 15-day breaks between sessions, the school offers intersessions to provide additional learning opportunities (extended time) for some 150 "off-track" students who are between 12-week regular school sessions.

Emerson serves about 800 students. Seventy-seven percent of these students are minorities, and 90 percent qualify for the free lunch program. The school views itself as a community of learners and strives to integrate its activities with the surrounding community, exposing the students to relevant life experiences whenever possible.

In addition the school offers English as a second language, Chapter 1 reading program, group and individual counseling, and a literacy program. Emerson houses a pre-kindergarten and a Chapter 1 program for four-year-olds.

Although the school district is reevaluating the year-round schedule, Emerson wants to maintain its year-round calendar (at least a single-track schedule) because the staff and administrators are convinced that it provides continuous uninterrupted learning for students.

The program began in September 1989.

(Contact: Anna Marie Ulibarri, Emerson Elementary School, 620 Georgia S.E., Albuquerque, N.M. 87108, 505-255-9091)

REORGANIZED DAY

Piscataquis Community High School in Guilford, Maine, with 350 students, serves a small, rural industrial community. Classes are scheduled for double periods to offer students more opportunities for collaborative learning.

The school's Project 2000, an RJR Nabisco-funded program, also emphasizes small-group instruction and hands-on learning opportunities for all students. The number of nontracked, activity-based courses has increased.

Project 2000 emphasizes small-group instruction and hands-on learning opportunities.

Project 2000 is designed to prepare students and staff for life in the next century by implementing a program of coordinated and constructive change at the school level. The curriculum is based on Maine's Common Core of Learning, a statement of the knowledge, skills, and attitudes all Maine high school graduates should possess.

Project 2000 also includes the computer networking of classrooms, staff development opportunities, and the development of participatory and interdisciplinary learning activities. The program began in September 1991.

(Contact: Norman Higgins, Piscataquis Community High School, P.O. Box 118, Guilford, Maine 04443, 207-876-4625)

COMMON FACTS

Administrators, teachers, and other professionals in these schools, in addition to having a clear vision of the purposes of their school, appear to share underlying beliefs. Some of these commonalities include:

• a belief that all children can learn at a high level even though children have different learning styles and rates. This means that being fair doesn't always mean being equal; rather, each child should get what he/she needs. School staff reorganize their programs in order to have the flexibility to provide additional resources (especially time) as needed;

• the realization that social realities in the community can interfere with students' ability to reach their potential. In response to these realities, the schools have accepted the challenge of providing non-traditional services to families, with the ultimate goal of enhancing learning;

• strong leadership, a vision of what is possible and a willingness to try something new;

• the ability to reach out to the community for services that could be offered by community organizations through the school.

YRE Basics: History, Methods, Concerns, Future

by Don Glines

Most give credit for the concept of year-round education (YRE) to Bluffton, IN, 1904. Several do relate its beginning to "summer vacation schools" in 1870, while others cite that urban schools in the U.S. in 1840 operated 240–250 days. Though few students attended that total, schools were open year-round. Contrarily, rural schools usually functioned only two to six months, the result of weather, transportation, farm, and fiscal priorities.

As documented in *Year-Round Education: History, Philosophy, Future,* the records of the early 1900s describe programs is a variety of communities, including Newark, New Jersey (1912); Minot, North Dakota (1917); Omaha, Nebraska (1924); Nashville, Tennessee (1925); and Aliquippa (1928), and Ambridge (1931), Pennsylvania. They were begun for many reasons: Newark to help immigrants learn English and enable students to accelerate; Bluffton to improve learning and create additional classrooms; Minot to meet the needs of the "laggards"; Aliquippa and Ambridge for space; Omaha to offer continuous vocational training programs; and Nashville to improve the quality of education—all valid pieces of the puzzle.

One of the most noted calendar options was created by William Wirt, the superintendent who began the first YRE program in Bluffton. Moving to Gary, IN, he instituted the work-study-play school and the famous platoon system. At its height, this extended year, extended day, curriculum oriented, space saving plan, in conjunction with the work-study-play concept,

Paper presented at the annual meeting of the National Association for Year-Round Education (San Diego, California, February 12–16, 1994). © 1994 by Don Glines. Reprinted with permission.

was adopted by 240 communities. In Gary, from 1907–1937, almost continuously, the program was available 50 weeks a year, 12 hours a day, 6 days a week. The book, *The Great Lockout in America's Citizenship Plants,* documents this exciting prototype.

Wirt, along with Henri Weber in Nashville; Harlan Vanderslice in Aliquippa; John Beveridge in Omaha; Bennett Jackson in Minneapolis; and Addison Poland and Warren Roe in Newark, N. J., led the pre-1940 continuous learning philosophies prevailing at that time among the advocates. They paved the way for the "modern" or current year-round programs. For various reasons, the many early adoptions did not survive the late 1930 depression years, and the national uniformity needed during World War II. Though there were numerous efforts to renew the plans between 1946–1966, the concept was not reactivated until 1968–69–70 in communities in Missouri, Illinois, California, and Minnesota. The 1970–1990 resurgence years which followed initially were primarily mechanical calendar changes to generate space, though the education and community assets became better understood as the calendar variations spread across the nation. During the late 90s, the focus [has been on] on the total value of YRE.

> **Eventually, half of all new programs adopted the single track format.**

Increasing numbers of communities began to realize that it no longer was sensible to utilize billions of dollars worth of facilities only three-fourths of the months of the year, one-half of the days, and one-fourth of the hours. Through creative calendar planning, space was increased by 25, 33, or 50 percent, depending upon the selected configuration. Innovative secondary schools could expand a site by 100 percent. Enrollment was the original driving force, but there was a growing acceptance of the *education, employment,* and *lifestyle benefits.* Eventually, half of all new programs adopted the single track format, which saved no space or money, but did offer many personal and educational advantages. Additionally, modified calendars for specific regional needs became popular, as in Yosemite Park, where school vacations were during off-peak seasons in November and March.

High schools have been slow to join the movement, but the crowded conditions which are now reaching the secondary level are creating implementation plans in a number of states. It apparently will just be a matter of time. In several districts, there are increases in single track high schools to accommodate the elementary calendars and create educational opportunities year-round. It is no longer just large urban and suburban districts which are encompassing YRE. Smaller units, communities, and towns are adopting, too. A rural school built for 300 is just as overcrowded, usually from city migration, at 450, as is a large site of 2,000 when it reaches its overflow capacity. With all the new students, affected small districts do not have the money to keep pace with construction needs, and most do not have enough land at their existing sites for more portables. But small schools also benefit from the more continuous learning advantages of a single track.

Since the re-introduction of year-round education in 1968, most YRE communities have tried to offer the option for families of either the nine-month or year-round calendar. Choice has long been and still is the preferable way to implement the concept. However, as more and more districts reach the saturation point, and as financing becomes less and less available, an increasing number are turning totally year-round. Boards are now realizing that with space shortage, requiring YRE is no different than the policy of mandating a September to June calendar. Either way, some constituents are going to be inconvenienced. The nine-month calendar has for years been "wrong" for perhaps a majority of the working families. To create a win/win environment where different factions can be served, districts have modeled a plan where each school in the community offers a choice of either 12 or 9 months—a two-calendars-within-a-school plan. Now, as voluntarily more are selecting year-round, and as the region grows, increasingly the sites are converting entirely to YRE. However, the original format offers the best of all worlds where it is feasible. North Carolina began 18 districts with school-within-school options.

In moving toward year-round, air conditioning and outdoor heat have become issues in many communities. To respond, states are making efforts to provide a/c funds for warm climate schools which adopt multi-track programs. Beyond that, pioneers are encouraging the consideration of summer and winter hours. If during the winter period the school operates from 9–3, the summer hours may be from 7–12:30, with reduced snack and passing periods. On most days, the rooms are not too hot until midday; physical education programs can be conducted in the morning hours. With such a schedule, the students have the afternoon free to stay out of the sun, swim, study, rest or work. Aliquippa, Pennsylvania, conducted a mandated YRE program from 1928–1938, using "summer hours" before air conditioning; neighboring Ambridge followed the same format from 1931–1937. The Wilson School in Mankato, Minnesota, from 1968 to 1977 used this same plan. American schools in "always hot" countries as in the Caribbean Islands, where the buildings have only grille[s] for windows, follow this plan every September to June. Those that have tried this approach have found it generally successful. Even after air conditioning is installed, there is consideration for staying on summer/winter schedules, as people often adapt and find they prefer early morning school in the hot season.

> Educators no longer have the luxury of funding empty school buildings for three months.

Year-round does create space, and saves a growing state billions of dollars in construction—and in over construction—should a decline in enrollment occur in the early part of the 21st Century. On a three-track calendar plan, a school designed for 600 will hold 900, without portables; on a four-track arrangement, the same site holds 800; and on a five-track configuration, 720. Districts would then need build only 2 or 3, 3 or 4, or 4 or 5 projected schools. Multiplied by every facility and district in a state, the savings in land, utilities, insurance, construction, maintenance, and staff are of tremendously significant proportions. Fiscal experts are indicating that educators no longer have the luxury of funding empty school buildings for three months.

When planning YRE, youth serving agencies (Scouts, YMCAs), parks and recreation, police, churches/Bible schools, camping directors, child care providers, business managers, industrial employers, and, of course, all classified and certificated staff—not to forget students, parents, boards, and universities—must be included; they are all affected. Back to school sales are held in June; Bible schools operate 12 months; basketball, swimming and art programs are needed during the day in January; police need to know that students will be [indoors] at 10:00 a.m. in October; year-round day care is essential.

Hospitals, businesses, and industries cannot remain solvent with idle facilities and equipment—and neither can schools. The added costs of air conditioning, 12-month support staff, limited extended teacher contracts, and altered maintenance programs do not compete with the savings in buildings, busses, textbooks, desks, landscaping, insurance, and other such factors, according to the studies conducted to date. The Educational Cooperative of the University of California at Riverside has engaged in a major study to verify or refute these findings of the past 20 years of YRE experience.

Calendars can be used for single track (all students in the same group—all vacationing together), with intersessions for education and lifestyle benefits, or they can be multiple track to assist with the shortage of space. The most popular to date are illustrated in their multiple track form; they follow the same number of days for single track, but have only one group rather than the three to five necessary to increase enrollment capacity; modified formats can be tailored for specific communities.

Concept 6: This is a one hundred sixty-three day calendar (or 180 with overlap days), divided into six terms of approximately 41 days each. Students in three groups (A, B, C) attend two consecutive blocks, or 16 weeks, followed by eight weeks of vacation. As this is a three-track calendar, when A and B are in school, C is on vacation; therefore, a high school built for 2,400 will house 3,600. It is popular at the secondary level, though is also used in the elementary grades.

Modified Concept 6: The same calendar as Concept 6, except the units are divided into four weeks. Thus a student attends eight weeks, followed by four weeks of vacation. Popular at the elementary level, a school of 250 will house 375, or one of 800 will comfortably hold 1,200; some districts use the modified form for K–6 and the original form for 7–12.

60-20: A four-track (A, B, C, D groups) calendar where students attend three 60-day instructional blocks broken by three 20-day vacations. Popular at the elementary and middle school levels, this plan houses 33 percent more students; thus a facility constructed for 450 provides for 600. It also works for high schools, as will all calendars.

45-15: The same four-track as the 60-20, except students attend four 45-day periods, interspersed with four 15-day vacations/intersessions. Popular at the elementary level, it has been successfully used in the secondary schools. A site built for 750 will seat 1,000 or one for 2,100 will shelter 2,800.

90-30: Basically the same four-track plan as the 60-20 and 45-15, except students attend 90 days followed by a 30-day vacation. It is especially popular at the secondary level, but also is used at the elementary; a school of 1,500 can house 2,000.

30-10: Another four-track variation of the 90-30, where students attend 30 days and have ten off. This revolving door is repeated six times for each track to equal 180 days of school and 60 of vacation. A facility built for 400 will house 520.

60-15: Students attend 60 days followed by 15 days off-track. This provides a popular common three-week vacation for all students and staff. The disadvantage for some districts is that the 60-15 is a five-track plan (A, B, C, D, E groups), thus increasing the space by only 25 percent, or a school of 600 to 720, rather than 800 or 900, as in four or three-track calendars.

Orchard: A five-track 60-15 calendar is featured, as in the regular 60-15. However, in this plan, rather than rotate groups of 30 students with their teacher (the entire track class goes on vacation in most configurations), 20 percent of each classroom on each track go on a three-week vacation. A teacher may have 35 students assigned, but only 28 at one time—and only 28 desks and books. The teacher retains his or her own room, teaches 225 days, receives commensurate pay, and still has eight weeks of vacation days. The students rotate in and out in groups of seven each, or $1/5$ of any class size, thus increasing space by 25 percent. Four California districts operate this unique program; it was first developed in Utah.

Flexible All Year: This plan requires placing curriculum in smaller unit packages; usually a single track, it can save space by individually tailored vacations, so that approximately the same percentage is always out of school during each September to June, and in school June to September. It matters not when or for how long the family is away, as long as the space, staff, and student combinations match. Students finish the unit packages and begin new ones when they return—or continue the "package." It can be used in any school, but is particularly suited to continuation, alternative, and magnet schools.

Personalized Continuous Year: Developed at the Mankato State University Wilson Campus School, this is similar to the Flexible All Year, but instead of "packaging," curriculum is completely personalized and individualized. School is open 240 days; students may plug in or out anytime as desired; they create their own vacations. Like the Flexible All Year, it was originally designed for single track, but works well as a multiple track in the same manner as the Flex; vacations are scheduled through a "voluntary/mandatory" format when space is essential.

Four Quarter: The curriculum is divided into four 12-week blocks (fall, winter, spring, summer); students attend three of the four. On a mandated basis, this is a four-track system, saving 33 percent space, as in the other four-group configurations. It was once the original and most popular K–12 calendar and is still considered by districts, especially at the secondary level. A site built for 3,000 can hold 4,000 or a smaller one for 900 can accommodate 1,200. In a voluntary extended year form, it is being modeled in Buena Vista, Virginia.

Quinmester: This is another five-track system. The curriculum is divided into five nine-week blocks of time. Students attend four of the five quins. It is preferred by the secondary level, but can serve the elementary, too. It saves only 25 percent; thus a facility for 1,500 will increase to 1,875. It was one of the early calendars and pioneered in Florida.

Concept 8: The curriculum is placed into eight six-week blocks of time. Students attend any six of the eight to complete their 36 weeks, thereby providing two six-week vacation periods. By balancing the terms, schools can save 33 percent space, as this becomes another style of a four-track calendar. Constructed for 1,800, the site grows to 2,400. It has been used at the K–12 levels in California. *Concepts 12* and *16* are variations: 12 four-week blocks, or 16 3-week blocks, each equal the same 48 weeks.

25-5: Generally used for single track situations and more often in alternative programs, it can be used for multiple track. Students attend blocks of 25 days each to reach 175—and do five additional days through variations in the calendar or independent study. The 25-10 is another variation of the plan.

There are others—the 45-10, 30-5, 50-5, 50-10 which are variations of the 45-15, 30-10, or extended year or calendars customized for a specific program or community—but the ones outlined currently are most commonly used or discussed.

Schools in a district, or in a "feeder system," may use the same calendar, or two different ones, or even three or four. Though often desirable, a single calendar is not necessary. If the elementary staff greatly prefers one, and the secondary another, or if some elementary schools prefer Calendar X, some Y, and some Z, most combinations will match. There are several keys: (1) each needs to end by June 30—or the end of the common fiscal year, so that students transferring can do so at the beginning of the next; (2) the calendar must "overlap" in a manner that ensures that families with elementary, middle, and high school children can have a block of common vacation time; (3) the bussing routes must be able to be satisfied; and (4) the central office staffs must be able to live with the diversity of different delivery and attendance accounting periods.

> Though most districts are committing to solve space and finance problems, more continue to offer YRE because of its non-space benefits.

Though most districts are committing to solve space and finance problems, more continue to offer YRE because of its non-space benefits. Even if facilities and funding are a major concern, educators are learning to help convince the communities toward a calendar change by highlighting the other advantages for the majority of residents. Once accustomed to the multiple vacation plans, growing numbers prefer to stay on them, if given a choice, for the reasons of continuous learning, employment realities, lifestyle diversities, enhancing facilities, improving curriculum, expanding community options, people considerations, and personal choices.

There are common pros and cons which always are the center of debates when YRE is introduced to communities: PROS—enhances learning; teachers and students return from breaks refreshed and motivated; reduces discipline problems; better student and teacher attendance; reduces teacher stress;

provides time for student enrichment classes during inter-sessions; allows families to take vacations during other seasons and when vacation destinations are less crowded; allows children more time to spend with parents while siblings are in school; eases overcrowding and makes better use of facilities in multitrack schools; parents with seasonal jobs, or in the military, can choose a calendar that allows more time for the family to be to-gether; day care is sometimes easier to arrange when fewer children are out of school; teachers can work in their profession year-round by substituting in schools with different calendars; medical ap-pointments can be scheduled during breaks. CONS—change is difficult; parents must arrange day care during fall and spring breaks; there may be different schedules for elementary children and their older siblings; children of teachers might attend a school on a different calendar; in-service days for teachers are harder to schedule; working on an advanced degree during the summer can be difficult for teachers; summer vacation is shorter; getting students to study during summer might be dif-ficult; teachers with other summer jobs might object to the change; administrators and clerical staff in multitrack schools are often overworked; communication with parents is more dif-ficult in multitrack schools; families might not get their first choice for the preferred calendar; students in multitrack schools will miss some school events.

> Educators, including the leading year-round advocates, are still learning how to improve the programs.

Educators, including the leading year-round advocates, are still learning how to improve the programs. There are a number of sources to assist beginners, the first and foremost being con-tact with the veteran districts that have been on YRE for 10–20 years. They are willing to share their knowledge and experience and should be visited. Most have found that the best way to be-gin is to start early, small (but yet a critical mass), and on a vol-untary basis, to learn the mechanics before a space crisis arrives or attempting to mandate it. In the meantime, this approach provides optional voluntary calendar choices for parents. How-ever, several communities have successfully chosen to go "all at once" and adopt it districtwide. Both approaches will work, if carefully planned and humanely communicated and implemented with the public.

The need for new facilities is real, but districts are learning that YRE can be an excellent ally. Though first piloted in 1904, and used extensively the past 20 years, the concept is still in its infancy, when viewed from the year 2000. Most of the current methods will become obsolete; they are only transitions to the next decade. Future-oriented educational planners believe the nine-month calendar will become an instrument of the past when the people truly understand the facility, finance, education, employment, and lifestyle benefits of year-round education.

What does the future hold? Year-round education will expand. Most districts will begin by establishing more traditional calendars such as the 45-15 or 60-20. However, moving toward the year 2000, more will transition to flexible all-year and personalized continuous calendars, such as the one developed at the Wilson Campus School. But beyond, a new dawning will eventually occur, as communities consider such possibilities as those designed for the Minnesota Experimental City—250,000 residents with no schools—and the city as the living learning laboratory.

In the coming systems, learning will be lifelong. It will occur everywhere, for many learn on their own. Everyone will be important, regardless of how much they know, and authority will be shared by all. Education will truly be a continuous process and will be tailored to finally really meet individual needs. People can and will make decisions about what and how they should learn. They will form positive social networks on their own without formal schooling; they will create choices.

In the 21st Century, YRE will be dramatically different. Such absolute time arrangements as Concept 6 or the 60-15 will disappear. If technologists can place astronauts on Mars by 2015, then certainly educators can create far better continuous learning systems in the next 20 years. It is time to do the impossible; the possible is no longer working. The future is bright for year-round education.

YRE Rationale: Philosophy and Methods

by Don Glines

T
HE CONCEPT
Year-round education (YRE) helps people individually,
and society in general, by providing calendar, curriculum,
and family options which more closely fit the changing life-
styles, work patterns, and community involvements for large segments of the
population. Opportunities for continuous lifelong learning are becoming an
essential characteristic as the world edges
into the 21st Century. For the immediate,
wherever possible, YRE should be offered
as a choice. The current ideal is for a
school or district to offer both the nine-
month and year-round calendar plans as alternatives. If only
one time form is possible, there are a number of reasons for
considering continuous education. YRE is based upon sound
philosophical rationale—upon concepts related to the quality of
life. It goes beyond year-round school (YRS), which is only a
mechanical scheduling system designed to house more students;
YRS does not consider the total learning environment. The potential for YRE far exceeds the possibilities for either nine-
month or year-round schooling.

> If only one time form
> is possible, there are
> a number of reasons
> for considering
> continuous education.

   Flexible, and especially optional, 12-month calendars can
be tailored to fit the personal needs and preferences of each
family unit by permitting vacation and other non-school activities to be scheduled throughout the year. Such a desirable goal

Paper presented at the annual meeting of the National Association for Year-
Round Education (Orlando, Florida, February 17–22, 1996). © 1996 by Don
Glines. Reprinted with permission.

is no longer theoretical, but practical, efficient, effective, and politically palatable, when properly understood and implemented. Continuous programs extend the learning opportunities available to all students by keeping school doors open more days of the year (usually 240, compared with 180), and by improving the learning choices in creative ways utilizing the summer climate months and multiple intersessions. They increase the resources available to society in three specific areas: human, physical, and fiscal.

The human aspect can be enhanced by enrolling only 66–80 percent of the students in the school buildings at one time, thereby leaving a potential pool of 20–34 percent of the youth throughout the year for voluntary service. Hospital candystripers, grandchildren for senior citizens, migrant student tutors, and other such badly needed personnel are among the possible contributions, while alleviating site congestion, or by providing optional vacation and learning schedules. William Wirt, Superintendent in Gary, Indiana, from 1907–1937 protested the closing of schools in the summer. He backed his convictions by keeping the Gary schools open free to all for 50 weeks a year, 12 hours a day, six days a week.

> The physical aspect of multiple track programs allows districts to consider fewer facilities.

The physical aspect of multiple track programs allows districts to consider fewer facilities. Precious land can be saved for more valuable ecological, park, and recreation use; the ongoing energy demands can be reduced; and the immediate drain on rapidly depleting raw materials can be relieved. Additional space can also be created for curriculum expansion. It does not make sense for community learning centers to stand empty for three months. Parents do not close hospitals (also helping institutions) for the same period.

The fiscal aspect can avoid unnecessary new construction; millions of dollars can be saved in growing communities. Long-term maintenance costs, and ongoing insurance and utilities fees can be reduced. In declining districts, older buildings may be closed sooner, preventing costly repairs and returning the structure and site to the community for new uses. Peak traffic reduction is a consideration in the crowded-freeway communities. Single track calendars do not save space or money, but, coupled with intersessions, they can offer continuous twelve-month learning.

Support is growing for YRE. In most districts, there is a 30-40-30 division of opinion when the concept is first broached. A minimum of 30 percent of the families will volunteer for a year-round calendar, 40 will be uncertain, and 30 will be opposed. Seventy percent is normally the maximum number of volunteers during the first and second years, though a few have reached 90; the average usually falls between 45–55 percent. Of the 30 most always opposed, 10–15 percent will be highly emotional, almost violently, against the plan. Some of the middle 40 will join the opponents when they are uncertain about how the proposal will affect them. The resulting early discussions of YRE leave a *minority* opposed, a *minority* uncertain, and a *minority* in favor. These figures can lead to conflict and win/lose schisms between voluntary and mandatory YRE proponents, and those who oppose any YRE adoption. Such splits in communities are unnecessary and contrary to the productive energy of the district, but divisions often occur where people do not comprehend the philosophy and purposes of YRE.

> Space should not be the driving force in establishing YRE; it is one of the side benefits.

IMPLEMENTATION

When first considering a change in school calendars, many leaders are searching for a way to alleviate overcrowding in classrooms and special facilities. Space should not be the driving force in establishing YRE; it is one of the side benefits. It is true that if districts are short of space, a continuous plan should be considered as one of perhaps five options: pass more bond and tax revenues and erect more buildings; double shift and/or extend the school day; initiate a voluntary YRE program and recruit enough participants to reduce the crowding; mandate a year-round calendar to create 25–35 percent more space, and thus, solve the enrollment problem; and mandate year-round and also build, sometimes a necessity in areas of rapidly increasing populations.

In space-cramped communities, mandating year-round education is acceptable when it is the best of the alternatives. Requiring YRE is no worse than mandating the present traditional nine-month calendar which is enforced in most districts. Comprehending this can lead to the 70 percent support, as the middle group will join the in-favor group to create an immediate solution to overcrowding. Unfortunately, the opponents of YRE are not willing to acknowledge the undemocratic aspects of the September–June calendar, and therefore continue to fight against the proposed year-round solution. The concept should not be the pawn in district space confrontations. Facilities use is not the prime justification for changing the calendar; the important reasons relate to program, people, choice, learning, and lifestyle. Therefore, year-round education should be offered as an option to all who could benefit, even if a district has a status quo or declining enrollment. If communities understand YRE as a philosophy, then the 20, 30, 40, 50, 60, 70 or 80 percent who volunteer should be allowed to implement a program.

Year-round education should be offered as an option to all who could benefit.

Imagine only 30 percent volunteering for the first year; that should be considered beautiful. The other 70 can remain longer in the traditional calendar; that is also beautiful, for both plans help people, which is the purpose of education. If a flexible year-round calendar can assist a *significant minority of the families,* then the district has the moral responsibility to provide such a program. It is a simple option to implement. It can be accomplished without additional, or only minimal, expense, and does not need to cause great conflict—certainly no more than having a variety of religious faiths sharing the community.

Related to curriculum, YRE on a voluntary, and more so on a mandatory basis, frees space for often needed additional special facilities such as art, industrial technology, home economics, drama, music, physical education, and resource centers. Most elementary schools were constructed with limited square footage designed for such programs. YRE multi-track in a full, but not overcrowded building, allows for conversion of rooms to these needs at no additional construction expense. In secondary schools at maximum capacity, YRE allows for expansion of space for these curriculum fields and reduces congestion in the hallways, cafeteria, gymnasium, library, lockers, and parking areas.

It is easy to envision, then, that YRE must be internalized philosophically for all its potential advantages to be understood, and to overcome any perceived or real disadvantages. Accepted as part of an educational philosophy, YRE should be available to all persons in a district, pre-kindergarten through adult, who could benefit, whether the community is growing or declining. Only in extremely small, rural districts may the option of YRE not be feasible, but even there, a mandated year-round program might provide more for the families than a mandated nine-month calendar. Most population centers, even of significant size, either do not offer YRE, or condone it only at the elementary, or in one section of the district, perhaps where it is overcrowded. They do not understand the philosophical intent of giving calendar and learning choices to all persons regardless of age level or the location of their home. YRE is an exciting option at all levels of learning. Fortunately, more educators are beginning to understand that it can and does work well in middle and high schools and colleges, as well as at the elementary and preschool ages.

> **YRE must be internalized philosophically for all its potential advantages to be understood.**

When YRE is mandated throughout the district, the schools focus on calendar and curriculum changes, but even in overcrowded situations, every effort should be made to create the availability of a nine-month calendar for those special need situations: health, extended travel, employment, and extenuating family situations. An Appeals Board can be established to function as the approval mechanism. To arrange for a traditional summer vacation, those limited numbers of exempt students can be allowed to jump tracks (when group A goes on vacation several of the students may transfer to group B, then to group C, and finally to group D). Sometimes a portion of a building, or one entire school, can be maintained on a conventional calendar. A continuous nine-month special plan can be used for any calendar period (as July through March), not just September to June.

In implementing the year-round concept within voluntary conditions, a number of organizational patterns have developed throughout the nation. They all work; one is not better than another. Four have emerged as the most popular and all are preferable to mandating, except in cases of extreme overcrowding. The first is the school-within-a-school plan. A number of sites offer both the nine-month and year-round options within the same building; some even refer to the selection as the single vacation and multiple vacation plans, rather than YRE, for an advantage of the voluntary choice is the selection of one longer vacation, or several shorter periods throughout the year. The second pattern is to pair geographically near schools, so that families have the preference of a neighborhood nine-month or year-round calendar. A third method is to create the "neighborhood cluster" where one of three or four buildings offers the option of a continuous year within the same calendar, such as is possible in the Concept 8, Flexible All-Year, and Personalized Plans.

> In implementing the year-round concept, a number of organizational patterns have developed.

METHODS

Creative districts offer families true freedom of choice, wherever YRE has been understood as a philosophy, not just a method of housing students or saving money. Districts that have begun year-round calendars and then later dropped them are among those guilty of not comprehending continuous life-long learning. They only see a mechanical way (YRS) to temporarily house an influx of students; they have not considered the 21st Century. Those energetic educators who have looked toward future learning delivery systems have been developing new varieties of calendar plans. No one scheduling arrangement has proven to be the best—only the most acceptable at this moment in time in a given location. YRE is still in the propeller stage in the majority of current efforts, but the jet and space ages of YRE have already been envisioned. The ideas are practical now when properly supported; needed for the future are "Voyager, Discovery, Endeavor, Columbia" style dreamers and doers.

For the present, over 30 different mechanical methods of rearranging the calendar toward continuous learning concepts exist: Staggered 45-15; Block 45-15, Flexible 45-15; Staggered, Block, Flexible 60-20; Staggered, Block, Flexible 90-30; Staggered or Block 30-10; 25-5; Concept 6; Modified Concept 6; Concept 8; Concepts 12 and 16; Multiple Access; Quarter Plan; Quinmester; 60-15; Orchard Plan; Extended School Year; Modified Summer Term; Flexible All-Year; Personalized Continuous Year; and many special community variations. They all work; they can all "fail."

> YRE has been criticized by those who administer very traditional group-paced education organizations.

Interwoven with these plans are the intersessions—student vacation periods and the year-round equivalent of summer school—but with a totally different perspective. They are considered a continuous part of the learning process, not isolated summer courses. The majority of students return for two or three enrollments (in a 45-15, they may take one or two of the three-week vacations, but they attend the other two or three intersession terms). Traditional, remedial, and enrichment opportunities are offered; more exciting are the creative, innovative curriculum options. Many are off-campus, community-centered alternatives, such as drama at the local theater, psychology at the mental health ward of the hospital, tent living and environmental studies in the mountains, oceanography at the sea coast, or pesticide studies on a farm. Parks and recreation activities, most sports, learning vacations (a study of the cavalry-Indian conflicts in Montana), year-round Bible schools, and community agency functions are available during the intersession periods, too.

YRE has been criticized by those who administer very traditional group-paced education organizations. They cite that in some smaller elementary schools teachers have been forced to accept two grade levels to balance the class enrollments. At the secondary, in small departmentalized programs, administrators have found it difficult to schedule singletons; teachers have insisted on rigid, but educationally indefensible prerequisites. This, again, is a matter of philosophy (YRE) versus mechanics (YRS)—of individuals who do not accept the rationale for continuous learning options for people, and alternative teaching styles. Ironically, part of the solution of these perceived dilemmas is to implement better educational practices. Those who volunteer for YRE will understand and want to create exciting programs. The advantages of non-graded, team taught, classrooms have been known for years, yet conventionally trained teachers have refused to examine the data. Seventh graders range from grade 3 to grade 13 on standardized achievement tests. Most grade levels have a plus or minus four-year span. Staff cannot argue for a seventh or fifth grade class when there truly are no such students. Even chronologically there is a gap of 12–15 months—and, further, not all students mature or progress on the same timetable. Physiologically, there is a six-year span for the seventh graders—some are pre-puberty "5th"; others are young adults (9th graders).

> **Good YRE programs purposely move toward non-graded learning modes.**

Good YRE programs purposely move toward non-graded learning modes. They also move toward individualization, especially at the secondary level, long proven to be more effective and feasible, at least in modified forms, if the methods are properly understood. Such an approach reduces the singleton/doubleton class dilemma. Students in a French class in most situations are spread from first through fifth year work, so they should just enroll in French, not French I or III. Some eighth grade English students write at fifth grade achievement standards and some at the 11th. Their instruction must be individualized; a common theme can keep a group working together as a class in English, not "eighth grade" English. Individualizing, non-grading, and teaming—each excellent instructional, philosophical, and mechanical approaches to learning—can be used to resolve the imagined dilemmas of combination and specialized classes. Similar changes can overcome other concerns, when there is a true commitment to lifelong learning. Such proposals are not wild, radical, impossible, or expensive. They can be implemented by caring educators. They are not experimental ideas; they are recipes proven over many years, as related through educational history.

THE RATIONALE

Though most districts are committing to YRE to solve space and finance problems, growing numbers are offering it because of its non-space benefits. Even if facilities and funding are a major concern, educators are learning to help convince the communities toward a calendar change by highlighting the people and societal advantages for the majority of residents. Once accustomed to a multiple vacation plan, most families prefer to remain on it, if given a choice. Eight reasons summarize the philosophical Rationale for Year-Round Education:

1. **Continuous Learning:** The concept that schools, like hospitals, are helping institutions and should never close, is gaining acceptance. Students should be able to learn in any of the 12 months; they should not, according to advocates, find a "closed" sign on the door in July. With creative use of intersessions, and rotating groups of students, there are always teachers available to help youth learn. Where facilities are too crowded to offer many intersession classes (vacation programs) on-campus, exciting use is made of many off-campus sites: parks, beaches, theaters, churches, art and music centers, mountains, swimming pools, zoos, business and industry laboratories, and portables.

2. **Employment Realities:** Construction workers, moving van drivers, farmers, baseball players, summer tourist operators, park rangers, those low on union seniority lists, and certain business employees, among others, cannot take summer vacations. Districts are learning that these parents appreciate non-summer periods to create time with their children. Further, teachers can increase their earnings through extended contracts, intersession employment, and substituting. Most outdoor workers in Minnesota need their vacation in January or February, not in July or August.

3. **Lifestyle Diversities:** States such as California have wonderful weather in September, October, April, and May. Those who can afford to travel usually prefer the desert in the spring, autumn leaves in the fall, and skiing in the winter. Districts are offering families three or four short vacations, rather than one long period. The calendar change has been called the "four-vacation plan" in several communities, rather than YRE. In many regions, combining employment and lifestyle prefer-

ences creates a majority who do not want schools closed June, July, and August. Swimming is still available during the summer break and with indoor pools, in the winter, too. Few families can take three consecutive months away from work; homelessness occurs in all 12 months.

4. **Curriculum Facilities:** Some districts that are full, but not overcrowded, are using YRE to create "elbow room." A school built for 900 can be reduced in on-site enrollment to 675 by a four-track calendar, thus freeing eight rooms to use for drama, art, computers, library, shops, or other special enhancements. A junior high of 1,600 can be reduced to 1,200, lessening crowds in the halls, library, lockers, gyms, special facilities, and cafeteria. Overcrowded schools can ease the crush on shops, rooms, labs, and outdoor space by reducing the numbers on campus each track.

5. **Improvement Catalysts:** Schools are also using YRE as a catalyst for restructuring. When adopting a continuous calendar, staff can consider Organization changes—nongrading; Curriculum options—individualization; Facilities—remodeling for elementary science; and Philosophy—more attention to the affective domain. Everything should be examined when considering a new calendar. Districts are finding that when properly implemented, year-round should improve the school. It opens the opportunity for change and innovation—and the transition toward 21st Century learning systems.

6. **Community Enhancements:** YRE has been enhancing communities through the adoption of twelve-month swimming lessons, park and recreation programs, and Bible schools; reduced highway congestion; less summer pressure on the police force; ongoing volunteers for health and social agencies; and continuous help for limited-English-speaking and special education youth. Preliminary evaluation has indicated that there is great potential for reducing the dropout rate and for increasing student skill and knowledge levels. Even gangs can be partially separated. Gifted students can pursue additional learning in specific areas of interest, while parents can be involved with learning year-round—true community schools.

7. **People Considerations:** The affluent can be concerned with skiing, vacations to Alaska, and private camp experiences.

But one of seven anglo, four of nine black, and three of eight Hispanic youth live in poverty. Forty million Americans are desperate, and many are homeless or extremely transient year-round; 39 percent are young people. YRE offers a "continuous home/role model" for part of most days every month, with breakfast, lunch, and snacks for a significant number of children in poverty. Those students who also attend intersessions receive services while on vacation, including efforts to address health and emotional as well as educational needs. Low-income families cannot take long trips, but with the variety of off-track periods, children can share at home whenever the parent can arrange a few days away from work or when unemployed. For those youth in "minimal home conditions," some relief may be possible daily by participating in year-round education. For others, hunting and fishing are options "in season."

    8. **Personal Choices:** Ideally year-round should be a win-win decision; both YR and nine-month learning should be offered as options. It should not be mandated unless essential, but it should not be denied those who benefit. If 49 percent want YRE, that is beautiful; if 51 percent can be helped by a September through June calendar, that is beautiful, too. It should not be win-lose. The 30-40-30 split that usually occurs when first proposed can be turned into a positive by caring educators. If YRE is implemented humanely, with considerations for all, it will be sanctioned by the majority. If a YR calendar must be mandated, provide nine-month options for those special individual family needs.

    Year-round is not new. It was offered in Bluffton, IN, in 1904 and Gary, IN, in 1907; Amarillo, TX, 1910; Newark, NJ, 1912; Minot, ND, 1917; Omaha, NE, 1924; Nashville, TN, 1925; Aliquippa, PA, 1969; St. Charles, MO, 1969; Valley View, IL, 1970; Chula Vista and La Mesa, CA, 1971. The National Association for Year-Round Education has been in existence three decades. If YRE can be understood as a philosophy, as a means for assisting the improvement of the quality of life for individual persons and for society as a whole, the concept will continue to grow as a viable alternative which can enhance the potential of learning and living communities. YRE, accepted in a win/win spirit, can personalize opportunities for all who choose to participate in the continuous programs which the concept can provide during the transition years into the 21st Century.

REFERENCES

Books

1. Glines, Don. *Creating Educational Futures: Continuous Mankato Wilson Alternatives.*

2. Glines, Don. *Year-Round Education: History, Philosophy, Future.*

3. Wirt, William and Glines, Don. *The Great Lockout in America's Citizenship Plants: Past as Future.*

4. Glines, Don. (Monograph). *Year-Round Calendar and Enrollment Plans.*

5. Winter, Walter. (Monograph). *Review of Recent YRE Student Achievement Studies (NAYRE).*

6. Hawkins, Sandy. (Monograph). *From Parent to Parent.*

Note: These 1995 publications are available from National Association for Year-Round Education (NAYRE), P.O. Box 711386, San Diego, CA 92111, (619) 276-5296.

7. Moffett, James. *The Universal Schoolhouse.* Jossey-Bass, San Francisco, 1994.

Videos

1. *The Wilson Experience.* (15 minutes). Performance Learning Systems, 224 Church Street, Nevada City, CA 95959, (961) 265-9066.

2. *Mankato Wilson Campus School Remembered.* (55 minutes). College of Education, Mankato State University, Mankato, MN 56001, (507) 389-1215.

Year-Round Education: Impact on Support Services, Transportation, Operation, Facilities, and Maintenance

by James C. Bradford Jr.

The real issue is not just adding or manipulating time, but changing the fundamental way we do business.—NEA-National Center for Innovation

Leadership and vision will be necessary if the educators of the 21st Century are to assure that each child in America has a viable future. The question is "are we truly serious about providing a world class education for each student?" The research has cited that the least successful schools have engaged in "shallow coping" (Lewis and Miles, 1990). The enemy of change is us; stated more succinctly by Oliver Hazard Perry in his message from the War of 1812: "We have met the enemy and they are [h]ours" (*Prisoners of Time*, 1994). The primary dilemma in organizational and system change is how to manage facility usage as related to the available hours in each available school day. School facilities are one of the most under-utilized components in the educational organization. The opportunities for educators in the educational organization are endless when finding ways to rediscover the hours available for reprogramming America's school facilities. It has been stated that an overwhelming number of

> School facilities are one of the most under-utilized components in the educational organization.

Paper presented at the annual meeting of the Association of School Business Officials of Maryland and Washington, D.C. (Arnold, Maryland, January 1995). © 1995 by James C. Bradford Jr. Reprinted with permission.

America's school facilities are only in use for a small percentage of the available time. The Nation's children are in need of an instructional schedule that provides more time for learning than the traditional 180-day agrarian calendar. Each local school administrator has a responsibility to effectively and efficiently manage the time utilization of a very costly educational resource—school facilities.

It is extremely difficult to draw a finite conclusion concerning specific dollar amounts when comparing the traditional versus the year-round operation.

As the public demands increase to make our educational programs more efficient and effective in an international and global society, the utilization of school facilities will become increasingly a subject for public debate. As increased organizational studies support maximum utilization of school facilities the term year-round education will seek new meaning. The task that befalls each educator is how to effectively and efficiently manage and utilize the available school facilities in an era when the time schedule of students has become one of national scrutiny. Individuals are mortal; however, individuals with great vision can solve the educational and facilities problems for student entry into the 21st Century.

FACILITY COSTS IN YEAR-ROUND SCHOOLS
During the past two decades, a number of studies have been conducted to determine if year-round schools are more costly to operate than the schools on the traditional agrarian calendar. Most of the earlier studies were based on hypothetical models, rather than the actual costs of placing a school on a year-round schedule. Many of the year-round schools have documented the operational costs. Due to many variables in calculating facility costs, it is extremely difficult to draw a finite conclusion concerning specific dollar amounts when comparing the traditional versus the year-round operation. According to a study conducted by school administrators in California (1988), a major variable in cost calculation occurs when several options are available. These include: year-round programs mandated in a school district for all the schools, voluntary for all schools within a district, mandatory with certain schools within a dis-

trict, voluntary with certain schools within a school district or voluntary within a district when parents make the choice between traditional and year-round schedules. Each option has a different effect on school facility costs. Additional complications in a study by Fardig (1992) stated that costs are determined and swayed by local policy decisions of the board of education and administration. Summer school, intersessions, and overtime for maintenance and custodial staff in multi-track schools (Stiff, 1986) are often given little attention when additional programs offered in some districts are not in other school districts.

> In multi-track year-round programs the issue of cost avoidance was the single most important concern in most of the studies.

The California school administrators (1988) determined that *single-track schools have little to no significant impact on costs.* District policy was the main cause when single-track school costs exceeded the traditional or agrarian calendar. School research from the Department of Business Services for Orange County Public Schools in Orlando, Florida (1994) revealed that school size was more influential on costs than the single-track calendar. When single-track schools of equivalent size were compared to single-track of similar size, the costs per student were not significant.

In multi-track year-round programs the issue of cost avoidance was the single most important concern in most of the studies. School divisions with limited funds and increasing enrollments have had to increasingly address the issue of capital costs as related to facility utilization. The Florida study (1990) cited the most commonly mentioned reason for establishing year-round multi-track calendars was in response to the public outcries for more efficient and effective utilization of the present facilities before launching costly new capital programs for constructing school facilities. The Parrish study (1989) reported that increasing a school's capacity to serve more students has become a political issue that requires informed actions. In a study by Fish and Taylor (1989), the report stated that the most commonly cited reasons for considering multi-track year-round education was the lack of financial resources and increased or uncontrolled growth in student enrollments. The Florida Department of Education (1990) reported that the most significant cost savings would be in the avoidance of new school construction costs. The study noted that gross operating costs would probably increase in schools converting to multi-track year-round programs; however, the report further stated the cost per pupil would probably decline in multi-track year-round schools. A study by Pettier (1991) stated that the operating cost on a per pupil basis in one of the most researched school districts in America (Oxnard, California) decreased by $130.00 per pupil in a multi-track schedule when compared to the traditional schedule in the same school district. Obviously, operating costs will increase when a multi-track school operates for 240–245 days rather than the traditional 180 days, but per pupil costs decrease, allowing a net savings to the taxpayer.

The study by the Department of Business in the Orange County Public Schools (1994) stated that there was no evidence to support that operating costs per pupil were higher in multi-track year-round schools than in those operating on a traditional calendar; however, there was significant evidence that indicated multi-track schedules may result in reduced per student costs. Further, placing traditional calendar elementary schools on a multi-track calendar and increasing the capacity by twenty-five percent enabled the school district to avoid twenty percent additional construction costs, or a construction cost savings of $2,432.00 per student.

The National Association for Year-Round Education in a study by Coleman and Freebern (1993) concluded that the decision to convert from a traditional schedule to a multi-track year-round schedule should be at the time a school's population exceeds 116 percent of its capacity. It is at the 116 percent that it would be advantageous to move from mobile units to a multi-track schedule.

CLASSIFIED EMPLOYEES COSTS IN YEAR-ROUND SCHOOLS

In a survey of one hundred thirty-eight classified employees by Rothberg, Ausherman and Preston (1994) of Orange County, Florida (custodians, food services, office staff and others—50 on single-track and 88 on multi-track), the response was that 88 percent of the single-track staff was very satisfied, satisfied, neutral; while only 50 percent of the multi-track personnel responded that they were very satisfied, satisfied, or neutral with their respective schedule. The Marion County Florida study (1988) noted that the operational cost was $22.00 less per pupil for students on the multi-track calendar when compared to students on the traditional calendar. Cost for custodial services on a pupil basis is essentially the same for year-round programs when compared to traditional schedules

> In the conversion from a traditional to a year-round calendar several advantages can be anticipated.

(Brekke, 1993). Normally, multi-track year-round operational costs are proportionate to the additional days of operation.

SCHOOL NUTRITION COSTS IN YEAR-ROUND SCHOOLS

In the conversion from a traditional to a year-round calendar several advantages can be anticipated: better utilization of facilities and equipment; smaller numbers of children when compared to a school operating at over-capacity, increased student meal participation, shorter serving lines, less crowding, and fewer discipline problems. According to a Marion County, Florida study (1988) it was noted that food costs were $4.00 per day less per student in the multi-track calendar when compared to students on the traditional calendar. The cost associated with school nutrition on a per meal basis should not vary significantly on the multi-track/single-track versus the traditional schedule. Staffing in school nutrition is based on the number of meals served. School nutrition workers prefer a twelve-month schedule. Federal funding is available on the same basis when the schools operate on extended schedules.

TRANSPORTATION COSTS IN YEAR-ROUND SCHOOLS

One of the considerations of converting to a year-round calendar is the possibility of increasing transportation costs. School bus drivers prefer a twelve-month schedule. In ideal situations the number of buses used can be reduced in proportion to the number of pupils served; however, if buses were to travel over similar routes without a reduction in miles or numbers of buses, the costs of such transportation will be increased. Oxnard, California (1986) noted a savings of 9.83% in transportation costs directly attributed to the multi-track year-round schedule with the elimination of four additional buses due to more efficient utilization of the present fleet. On a per pupil basis the costs of transportation will remain constant for pupils on traditional schedules when compared to students on a multi-track schedule (Brekke, 1987). The Marion County, Florida study (1988) noted that the transportation costs were the same for a multi-track calendar when compared to a traditional calendar. Visalia Unified School District in California reported that transportation costs remained constant on a per student basis when traditional schedules were compared to year-round schedules.

> Public debates are usually about start-up costs, not the long-term savings or expense.

CASE STUDY OF COSTS INCURRED IN DISCONTINUING A YEAR-ROUND MULTI-TRACK SCHOOL SYSTEM

After 14 years of operation in a division wide multi-track year-round school program with 78,000 students (1989) in the Jefferson County Schools, Colorado, the district had a real cost savings of $87.7 million dollars in bonded indebtness, without giving consideration to savings in the operational and support areas (White 1990). In August 1988, the Jefferson County School Board discontinued the school district's multi-track year-round program for political reasons. What was the cost to the taxpayer for the discontinuation? This is a question that is usually omitted from the heated discussions in public debate about the costs of implementing year-round schooling. The public debates are usually about start-up costs, not the long-term savings or expense of program termination as was the case in Jefferson, Colorado. Unknown to the school board at the time of the multi-track termination were the start-up costs of $87.7 million dollars in increased bonded debt for eight new schools, plus the added operating costs of $6.6 million required for opening six new elementary schools and two new high schools because of multi-track schedule discontinuation and increased instructional costs of $1.9 million dollars. The "reality check" for the school board's decision to discontinue the year-round multi-track schedule totaled $116 million dollars in additional costs to the district to house the same number of students.

In 1974, when Jefferson County introduced multi-track year-round education, the objective was to save on building costs and increase the capacity of each school facility in a rapidly growing school district with limited resources. Admittedly, the school board did not have the exact figures on how much money was actually being saved in the operation of the year-round multi-track program in Jefferson County Schools. Little consideration was given to the additional funding required for the increased operational costs, textbook costs, capital costs, interest costs, and other costs necessitated in bringing six new elementary schools and two new high schools into the district budget.

Other considerations omitted were the unexpected negative public reaction to the school board decision to discontinue the multi-track schedule. The school board decision promulgated a vote of no confidence by teachers because of the increased operational and capital costs that deferred or stalled teacher raises (1988). The superintendent found himself in an impossible situation and retired (1988). Two board members did not seek reelection and one was defeated at the polls. The new board had to increase property taxes. The taxpayers rejected the tax increase for the increased operating expenses and increased capital improvement program (1989). The taxpayers revolt was evident at the ballot box. A survey of the residents revealed that eight percent of the residents wished to end year-round schools.

CONCLUSION
The nation's schools are facing many problems, one of which is the decaying, overcrowded, poorly maintained, and obsolete school facilities. Over 50 percent of the school facilities in use today were built in the 1950s and 1960s. According to a national report, "Wolves at the Schoolhouse Door: An Investigation of the Condition of Public School Buildings," many were built hastily and as cheaply as possible. The condition of America's school facilities represents one of the many financial problems that will become an integral component in the restructuring of education for the 21st century child. America's children, like its

school facilities, have been basically ignored in many states and school districts by the legislatures, the electorate, the school officials, and the school board due mainly to limited financial resources. The literature reveals that the break even point in cost for a school board moving to a multi-track year-round program is when a school's enrollment exceeds 116 percent of its stated (facility) capacity. Students housed in a facility exceeding 120 percent of capacity probably will generate both an operational and capital savings. A study of six school districts by Coleman and Freebern (1993) stated that when building capacity was under and up to 110 percent, mobile units were less expensive than initiating multi-track. When the enrollment capacity was 116 percent and higher, a multi-track year-round program was fiscally prudent.

Year-round education is a concept that has been in existence for approximately 100 years. A number of single-track and multi-track school districts have been successfully utilizing year-round school calendars for over twenty-five years. Year-round multi-track education schedules provide a viable option to school construction that accommodates periods of rapidly increasing students enrollments when financial resources are limited. The single-track programs offer a cost effective means of increasing educational programming for promotion, remediation, enrichment, and acceleration. Some year-round programs are reducing the number of repeaters, which is cost effective. Other programs for enrichment will require additional funding. One cannot argue that vacant hotel rooms, vacant hospital rooms, and vacant classrooms from June to September is an efficient and effective use of facilities. Well-designed year-round schedules can reduce facility costs and produce educational programs of quality.

Year-Round Education

by Sue E. Mutchler

Year-round education addresses two key problems: the need to use present school facilities most efficiently in districts with growing student populations and the need to maximize student learning outcomes, particularly for students with special needs. In the former case, districts that experience a combination of overcrowded schools and taxpayer refusal to pass school bond proposals or raise taxes are turning to year-round education as a means of accommodating more students in existing school facilities. In the latter case, year-long services have been available for special education students for a number of years, based on the belief that continued instruction during the summer months reduces students' skill loss. Proponents of year-round education state that it makes the most of learning time for all students: those students achieving at the norm as well as at-risk students, gifted and talented students, and students with disabilities.

> Proponents of year-round education state that it makes the most of learning time for all students.

    The number of year-round schools in the United States has ebbed and flowed. After a number of experiments in the early 1900s ended, the concept lay dormant until the late 1960s. By 1976, more than 600 schools in 28 states operated on year-round schedules. By 1980 they had declined to 287 schools, but another resurgence of interest brought the number to more than 1800 schools in 26 states by 1992. Ninety percent of these schools were located in three states: California, Nevada, and Utah. Texas was behind only California in terms of numbers of

From *SEDL Insights*, no. 2, March 1993, pp. 1–3, 5–6 © 1993 by SEDL. Reprinted with permission.

students served in such schools. The vast majority are elementary schools, which appear to adapt to the scheduling demands more readily than secondary schools (Carriedo & Goren, 1989).

MECHANISMS FOR LOCAL IMPLEMENTATION

Districts can implement year-round education programs in a number of different ways (Merrell, 1980). Each of the following mechanisms responds to a particular set of district needs and objectives.

Pilot Schools

One school or one set of feeder schools (i.e., a high school paired with its students' junior high and elementary schools) is selected to implement a year-round program. This model includes magnet schools that offer specialized programs centralized in one school and allow students from throughout the district to attend.

Schools-Within-a-School

A year-round calendar and a nine-month calendar are both offered in the same building, with a portion of the student body attending each.

Plan-Within-a-Plan

Both calendars are offered in the same instructional program. For example, a year-round schedule that organizes the entire school's curriculum in six-week units enables "families that desire the nine-month calendar [to] choose the six six-week periods that fall between September and June. Those wishing a year-round calendar can select any of the eight six-week periods" (Merrell, 1980, p. 44).

Paired and Clustered Schools

In larger districts, neighborhood schools are paired or clustered into groups of three or four. One or more offers a year-round schedule while others offer the traditional nine-month plan.

Schools can select from a wide variety of year-round scheduling plans: the 45-15 plan (45 school days attendance followed by 15 school days of vacation); the similar 60-20 plan; the

60-15 plan (which provides a common July vacation for all tracks); the Concept 6 plan (six terms of 43 days each); the Concept 8 plan (eight six-week blocks); the quarter plan (four twelve-week periods); the quinmester plan (five nine-week terms); and a number of flexible plans. In 1992, the most common schedules were 90-30; 60-20; 45-15; 60-15; and Concept 6. There were no Concept 8 schools, and fully half of all year-round schools were single-track. Each scheduling plan has the potential to provide opportunity for learning benefits to students; multi-track arrangements also can increase school capacities by 33 percent or more (Merrell, 1980). Again, the district's particular needs and the community's preferences will guide the selection of a specific scheduling and tracking plan for year-round education.

> The district's particular needs and the community's preferences will guide the selection of a specific scheduling and tracking plan.

IMPLEMENTATION BENEFITS AND DIFFICULTIES

Proponents and practitioners state that year-round education brings fiscal relief to the district, positive educational outcomes to students, and additional benefits to the school community as whole. Among these are:

- more efficient use of school facilities (e.g., use throughout the school year, less need for new buildings and/or higher taxes, conservation of fuel);
- improved student and teacher attendance;
- fewer student discipline problems;
- less stressful teaching conditions;
- greater career flexibility (e.g., extended teaching contracts, cross-track or specialized teaching) and increased salaries for teachers who teach throughout the year;
- more diversified, enriched curriculum and instruction;
- remediation or acceleration opportunities for special needs students during vacation intersessions;
- greater retention of learning for all students (i.e., less learning loss during breaks between school sessions/years);
- accelerated completion of graduation requirements;
- increased learning time for disadvantaged [and] gifted students;

• decreased school dropout rates due to expanded remedial instruction and re-entry opportunities in the school
system; and
   • less vandalism in schools.

A number of implementation difficulties also have been reported. Many of these are management problems that might be
expected with the introduction of any new organizational design, and most appear in schools that implement multi-track
programs. The literature reports problems in the following
areas:
   • coordinating the school schedule with student teacher
schedules (though the addition of a summer quarter for student
teaching seems to offset this difficulty);
   • coordinating multi-track schedules in secondary schools;
   • coordinating schedules for families of students attending
different schools;
   • scheduling meetings for school personnel in multi-track
schools;
   • maintaining a unified effort for both staff and parents;
   • accomplishing long-term planning for the instructional
program;
   • transition difficulties (e.g., curriculum changes when
schools switch from 9-month to year-round, lack of support for
teachers on different tracks in adapting to such changes as sharing rooms and storing materials);
   • administrator fatigue in multi-track schools;
   • parent objections; and
   • start-up expenses and modifications to existing buildings
to accommodate a multi-track year-round program.

POLICYMAKING CONSIDERATIONS
In considering the feasibility of encouraging or mandating the
implementation of year-round schools, policymakers will want
to address three sets of questions (Burnett, 1979):
   1. How do single-and multi-track year-round education
programs compare with traditional-calendar education in terms
of capital, operating, and start-up costs, both in the short term
and long term?

2. Will the year-round schedule affect student achievement? If so, how?

3. What attitudes will students, parents, teachers, and community members have toward the program? Will attitudes change?

Answers to the first two questions require up-to-date information from schools and districts currently implementing year-round programs. Policymakers will want to consider both fiscal impact and student achievement outcomes over time. The third question has implications for the policy guidance that is needed to enable districts to implement year-round education successfully. The following sections present some of the available research results in these three areas.

> A multi-track program produces overall operational savings as well as capital savings.

Fiscal Impact

A cost analysis of nine school districts in California, Illinois, and Virginia concluded that careful implementation of a year-round school program can result in substantial cost savings" (Burnett, 1979, p. 29). A multi-track program produces overall operational savings as well as capital savings. Burnett asserted that long-term costs and benefits of implementing year-round education can be accurately analyzed only by comparing the existing situation at a school with a simulation of the situation under the proposed calendar (i.e., the population, pupil/teacher ratio, curriculum, etc. must be held constant). His rationale for using such an evaluation method is to control for two common types of expenditure that should be external to a true comparison of economic impact: (1) the transition to a multi-track year-round education program requires additional start-up costs, and (2) the year-round education program typically serves as a catalyst for many changes not related to the program—changes that bear costs of their own. Burnett suggested that the most important policy and planning variables related to long-term cost are: staffing ratio, construction costs, classrooms not used for basic instruction, and teacher compensation.

Changes in any of these variables can reduce or increase savings significantly.

An example of how dramatic these changes can be is found in Houston, Texas. The final 1984–85 evaluation report for the year-round schools in Houston, Texas, stated that the cost of converting schools to year-round represented a 33.8% increase in the average cost per pupil (Guthrie, 1985). However, in addition to incurring start-up costs, the district implemented some costly intersession programs. These programs may account for more of the cost increase than did conversion. Further, costs can decline radically in the program's later years. For example, in the second year of implementation, one of the Houston schools showed only a 6.7% increase in the average cost per pupil while traditional elementary schools in the district showed an 8.5% increase.

Evaluators found greater achievement gains in the year-round program.

Changes in Student Achievement

While research is not conclusive about the speed at which positive outcomes occur, a number of changes in student achievement can nevertheless be reported. The Houston evaluation report concluded that the dominant successes of the year-round education program focused on educational benefits (Guthrie, 1985). Evaluators found greater student achievement gains in the year-round program. A comparison of student scores on the Iowa Test of Basic Skills (ITBS) before and after they attended a year-round school showed a composite average normal curve equivalent (NCE) gain higher than a sample of students who continued to attend a school with the traditional schedule. Furthermore, the mean gains for students in the year-round school were significantly different from the comparison schools. Evaluators cautioned that results of any first-year program should, of course, be viewed conservatively; and some believe that Houston's intensive intersession programs, rather than the year-round education program itself, may have produced these gains.

San Diego Unified School District released a longitudinal report in March 1991 comparing test scores in traditional and year-round schools from spring 1982 through spring 1990. Results of the Comprehensive Test of Basic Skills (CTBS) for grades 1–6 and the California Assessment Program (CAP) for grades 3 and 6 were included (Alcorn, 1991). The report revealed significant differences in the percentage of year-round schools that maintained or improved student scores compared to the results for traditional schools. The average percent change in scores was also significantly higher in year-round schools. For example, grade 5 showed:

• 59% of traditional schools maintained or improved CTBS reading scores, with an average percent change of +1.0.

• 81% of year-round schools maintained or improved CTBS reading scores, with an average percent change of +7.3.

There appears to be a difference in performance between types of year-round schools, as well. For example, grade 3 showed:

• 60% of traditional schools maintained or improved CAP reading scores, with an average percent change of +4.6.

• 68% of year-round schools maintained or improved CAP reading scores, with an average percent change of +14.3.

• 80% of multi-track year-round schools maintained or improved CAP reading scores, with an average percent change of +18.5.

Other current reports of the positive impact of year-round education on student achievement include the following:

• A state-wide evaluation of Utah's year-round and extended-day schools by Brigham Young University, under contact with the Utah State Department of Education (Van Mondfrans et al., 1989);

• A comparison of CAP scores in the Oxnard School District, Ventura County, California, with state CAP scores (Oxnard School District, 1989). The report examines gains over a six-year period.

• An eight-year study of student ITBS scores at Willow Canyon Elementary School in Sandy, Utah (Willow Canyon Elementary School, 1990). The report compares four years under the YRE program with the previous four years under the traditional calendar.

Impact on Local Constituents

A report by the Utah Foundation stated that year-round education clearly has an impact on families through the demands it makes on family lifestyle (e.g., child care arrangements, coordination of siblings' schedules, vacation plans, participation in other traditional summer activities). The report asserted, however, that the major difficulty is in combatting "the prejudice against the program that exists in the public mind in places where the system never has been used" (Utah Foundation,

Stiff resistance can be expected unless the advantages of the program are discussed early on.

1985, p. 224). Stiff resistance from parents and some business communities can be expected (in Texas, for example, summer camp owners have voiced opposition) unless the advantages of the program are discussed early on and efforts are made to respond to such concerns prior to program implementation.

A report by the Utah State Board of Education offered the results of an extensive examination of alternatives to school building construction, including year-round education (Merrell, 1980). A number of the report's conclusions and recommendations focused on the public's resistance to alternatives to school building construction, stating that such alternatives are "perceived as requiring major changes in the traditional lifestyle of parents, families, and educators [and the entire community]" (Merrell, 1980, p.47). Specific findings included the following:

• Implementation of year-round education may affect employment patterns, recreation needs, and church and community activities if a sizable number of schools change schedules or calendars. For example, businesses that have traditionally depended on high school workers who can work part-time hours and summers will have to significantly alter how they use this work force, or find a different source of labor.

• *Mandated* year-round school programs have less chance of success than do programs introduced as *options* to the traditional programs. If mandate is necessary, "the degree to which the public is involved in the determination of the mandated program seems to be the key to the success of the program."

• Year-round education programs work best when a high school and all its feeder schools participate in the same program, allowing all children in the same family and neighborhood to be on the same schedule or calendar. This is also a concern for teachers who want their own children to be on their schedule.

• Adoption and implementation of any alternative chosen requires careful planning and the involvement of parents, students, and educators if it is to be successful.

Local districts also will need to ensure responsiveness of central office departments to the unique needs of year-round schools. The Houston school district reported that the dominant implementation problem cited by principals and coordinators was the difficulty in working with central office departments. The latter, particularly the pupil accounting, personnel, and testing departments, had problems adjusting their planning capabilities and services to a new and different calendar (Guthrie, 1985). Further, the state education agency may need to alter certain procedures to accommodate year-round education.

CONCLUSION

Year-round education is an increasingly attractive concept for state and local policymakers who are seeking new ways of addressing either of two very different problems: (1) how to accommodate growing student populations in a climate of shrinking funds for school construction, or (2) how to improve student learning outcomes. Depending on whether year-round scheduling is single- or multi-track, it can provide additional space in current facilities to meet the first need and can provide additional learning time in each calendar year of schooling to meet the second.

As policymakers consider the viability of the concept for their state or district, they will want to consider the following issues:

• philosophic and demographic reasons for implementing the strategy;

• the local context within which year-round education will be promoted, and may be resisted;

- specific options for scheduling and implementation;
- cost estimates and comparisons;
- implications for special student populations (at-risk and gifted/talented, early childhood/day care, students with disabilities); and
- methods of evaluating the program and student outcomes.

Policymakers will want to consider the interrelationships between these issues. For example, in weighing the strengths and weaknesses of year-round school scheduling options, they will want to assess how the various models and tracking arrangements fit the economic and demographic needs of the district or state. Any year-round education model has potential for improving instruction and student outcomes, but a multi-track model is needed only if the district or state is also experiencing an economic and growth environment that demands space efficiency. Policymakers also will want to examine options for implementing the selected model district-wide, to look at long-term economic costs and potential educational benefits to all children in a particular locality.

There are research findings, though limited, that suggest year-round education brings fiscal relief to the district, positive educational outcomes to students, and additional benefits to the school community and learning environment as a whole (e.g., more satisfied teachers, improved curricula). As state and local policymakers consider the feasibility of implementing a year-round school model in their districts, they will want to compare actual outcomes documented by year-round schools with those of traditionally-scheduled schools. There is research support for the following conclusions:

1. The *fiscal implications* of year-round schools are not as simply drawn as once thought. Implementation yields savings in classroom construction, but these savings are tempered by two sources of additional costs: conversation of schools to accommodate multi-track year-round scheduling (i.e., initial start-up costs) and implementation of other school changes not related to but inspired by the shift to a year-round model (e.g., costs associated with intersession activities), Another source of savings, however, is found over time; research suggests that, af-

ter the initial year of implementation, the average cost per pupil of operating a year-round school is lower than that of operating a traditionally-scheduled school.

2. Both first-year and longitudinal evaluations of *student achievement* suggest greater gains on standardized achievement tests (e.g., ITBS, CTBS, and the California Assessment Program) in year-round schools. Differences are found among types of year-round schools as well, with the highest scores and greatest percent change found in multi-track year-round schools when compared to the total performance of all year-round schools.

3. Converting schools to year-round scheduling has a significant *impact on families and communities* that must be considered in order to gain public support rather than resistance to implementation. A new school schedule directly affects family life outside of schooling, which then produces a domino effect in other community sectors. Theses impacts need to be factored in during the exploration and decision-making processes to ensure community buy-in and a smooth implementation.

BIBLIOGRAPHY

Alcorn, R. (1991). *Comparison of test scores: traditional and year-round schools, comprehensive test of basic skills (grades 1–6) and California Assessment Program (grades 3 and 6).* San Diego, CA: San Diego Unified School District.

Ballinger, C. (1988). Rethinking the school calendar. *Educational Leadership, 45*(5), 57–61.

Barrett, M.J. (1990, November). The case for more school days. *The Atlantic Monthly,* pp. 78–106.

Brekke, N.R. (1992, May). Year-round schools: An efficient and effective use of resources. *School Business Affairs,* pp. 26–37.

Burnett, R.W. (1979, April). *A year-round school cost model.* Paper presented at the annual meeting of the American Educational Research Association, San Francisco.

Carriedo, R.A., & Goren, P.D. (1989). *Year-round education through multi-track schools.* San Francisco, CA: Far West Laboratory for Educational Research and Development.

Guthrie, T. (1985). *Year-round schools final evaluation report, 1984–85.* Houston, TX: Houston Independent School District.

Merrell, R.G. (1980). *A report on alternatives to school building construction.* Salt Lake City, UT: Utah State Board of Education.

National Association for Year-Round Education. (1991). *Eighteenth reference directory of year-round education programs for the 1991–92 school year.* San Diego, CA: author.

O'Neal, S., Alexander, B., Seidenwurm, J., & Weil, K. (1991). *Year-round education: The second year, 1990–1991.* Albuquerque, NM: Albuquerque Public Schools.

Oxnard School District. (1989). *YRE and academic achievement.* (Available from the Oxnard School District, Ventura County, CA.)

Utah Foundation. (1990). *Evaluation of year-round schools in Utah* (Research Report Number 530). Salt Lake City, UT: author.

Utah Foundation. (1985). *Year-round schools in Utah* (Research Report Number 459). Salt Lake City, UT: author.

Van Mondfrans, A., Moody, J., & Walters, L. (1989). *Statewide evaluation of year-round and extended-day schools: Executive summary.* (Available from Utah State Office of Education, Salt Lake City, UT.)

White, W.D. (1990). *New cost savings discovered in year-round schools.* (Available from National Association for Year-Round Education, San Diego, CA.)

Willow Canyon Elementary School. (Feb. 8, 1990). *YRE conference report.* (Available from Willow Canyon Elementary School, Sandy, UT.)

Section 2

Year-Round Education: Examples at Work

Nothing can take the place of practical experience out in the world.
—A. B. Zu Tavern

While the opening section provided general information about year-round education, this second group of articles moves the investigation directly to the specific sites that exemplify schools utilizing year-round education structures. The five studies presented in this section represent the various levels of schooling, from kindergarten through college. Four of the selected articles offer a look at year-round education models tailored to fit the particular circumstances of a community or district; the other actually cites a number of schools and their particular findings. Each, however, presents a prototype that can be modeled or reshaped according to the pertinent needs of schools considering the move to year-round schooling. Together, the five articles provide a rich source of practical ideas for schools to draw on.

Piper writes about a Catholic elementary school nestled near Honolulu in which the principal describes year-round education as "participatory education at its highest level." Citing a brief history of year-round education and the emergence of year-round schooling, particularly in the Pacific region, the author describes a hybrid, 45-15 schedule adopted by the Star of the Sea School. The principal advises that, although in her situation she "pushed" the plan through, it is wise to involve the entire community in the decision-making process. In closing, the article cites not only the improved test scores in reading, writing, and math, but also points out the many benefits of the "continuous flow" for students. Closing with the assertion that "the school calendar is a calendar of possibilities," Piper mentions some of the drawbacks experienced and points out valid feedback from parents.

In another example, which highlights a high school in an industrial community in Virginia, Bradford cites the national Governor's Association and their publication, "Time for Results." Basing his argument on the proposition that it "makes no sense to keep closed half a year the school buildings in which America has invested a quarter of a trillion dollars while we are under-educated and over-crowded," the author makes his case for year-round education as a practical way to meet educational needs in an informational, technological, and global society. He goes on to say that secondary schools must develop a plan that restructures curriculum so that it teaches students rather than courses. Citing many of the benefits of year-round schooling, Bradford delineates the process of change for Buena Vista High School, from endorsements and approvals, to program changes and fiscal considerations. In a comprehensive evaluation of the four-quarter system, the positive results are summarized in the reasons why over 50 percent of the students at this school choose to attend year round—promotion, enrichment, acceleration, remediation. This exemplary model has been cited by more than twenty state and national publications and has received a number of prestigious awards for excellence in education. Because of its long history as a year-round school, Buena Vista certainly warrants attention by those considering year-round education.

Campbell presents another elementary school example, but this particular institution targets academically at-risk students. A controlled study, in which both qualitative and quantitative data are collected and analyzed, suggests that year-round schooling "may not significantly improve outcomes for all students in all circumstances. However, if the qualitative perception data are considered, it appears that the calendar configuration can contribute to student and parent morale, as well as decreasing teacher burnout."

Inger, in a brief but informative essay, cites not one but a number of schools in California and Colorado that have found year-round education to be a viable and cost-effective solution to the problem of overcrowded schools. Inger cites Oxnard Unified, Pajaro Valley, and San Diego Unified as examples of year-round schools that have experienced positive results. The author also mentions Cherry Creek District 5 and Riverside Unified School District and the mixed results of their parent/teacher/student surveys. In sum, parents talked about the impact on family vacations and the availability of child care; teachers liked the more frequent breaks, but were concerned about continuing their own education; and students generally favored year-round schooling.

In the final article of this section, a college example of a year-round school is profiled. Cash et al. present the case of Western State College of Colorado and its 3 month-2 month-3 month-2 month year-round calendar. Stating that the intent of the schedule is to reorient the institution from a teacher-centered to a learner-centered community, the authors discuss the roles and relationships that have emerged out of the calendar change. The new schedule changes the curriculum by affording opportunity for a variety of pedagogical approaches, particularly for freshman studies. In addition, the change in scheduling necessitates a reconfiguration of classrooms in order to accommodate a more interactive teaching style. Brief and to the point, the article touches on some substantive ideas that lend insight into a college-level prototype for year-round education.

Year-Round Schools:
The Star of the Sea Model

by Paul S. Piper

Star of the Sea School had its share of challenges, from its humble beginning in 1946 to its current role as a school that shines brightly as a model for other Pacific schools. Nestled in the Wai'alae-Kahala area of Honolulu, Star of the Sea, a private Catholic K–8 school, sparkles with enthusiastic and creative energy. This is clearly a place where things are happening. Exciting things.

Star of the Sea's principal, Darla DeVille, has been a proactive force by applying cutting-edge educational research. Her vision of year-round schooling (YRS) has provided the school a new direction, and a new lease on life. Previous to YRS, Star of the Sea had problems that needed immediate attention: enrollment was slipping, community and school spirit was waning, and in 1989 the high school closed.

> Year-round schooling is not merely going to school all year, but rather is "participatory education at its highest level."

To Darla, year-round schooling is not merely going to school all year, but rather is "participatory education at its highest level. It allows students, parents and teachers the flexibility to provide quality education within the core curriculum, while maintaining a high level of academic excellence. It provides the entire community an opportunity to continue to learn and grow together on a year round basis."

From *Educational Innovations in the Pacific*, vol. 1, no. 1, May 1994, pp. 1–4.
© 1994 by Pacific Region Educational Laboratory. Reprinted with permission.

Darla DeVille deeply believes in the ability of year-round schooling to enhance student/teacher attitudes, community involvement, student performance, and the curriculum. She uses year-round schooling to unify many facets of educational theory and practice into a cohesive philosophy of education.

Discovering the concept while attending graduate school at the University of Wisconsin, Madison, she researched the subject thoroughly, used it, and became a firm believer in its power to transform schools. When she was hired by Star of the Sea they were losing enrollment. Now, three years later, they have gained over one hundred new students, successfully engaged a high level of community support, created a space during intercessions for unique and exciting classes, raised money with intercession classes, and created almost unparalleled school spirit. Year-round schooling is obviously much more than going to school all year long.

During the early twentieth-century there were many examples of year-round education.

HISTORY OF YEAR-ROUND SCHOOLS

The idea of year-round education is hardly new. In 1645, in Dorchester, Massachusetts, children attended school all year, for the first seven months from 7:00 a.m. to 5:00 p.m., and for the last five months, giving them a respite, 8:00 a.m. to 4:00 p.m. Year-round schools became relatively popular during the 1800s, particularly for the purpose of assimilating immigrant children into the American culture more quickly (Zykowski, Mitchell, Hough, & Gavin).

During the early twentieth-century there were many other examples of year-round education. These experiments were undertaken in order to address a number of concerns including overcrowding, financial problems, and declining academic achievement. These models became the precursors of the systems we have today. In the 1960s, in order to combat rising costs and enrollments, and to better utilize school facilities, the school district of Valley View, Illinois, piloted a 45 days on, 15 days off plan (often referred to as 45-15). This plan, and slightly modified versions of it, has become the most prevalent model of year-round schooling to date.

By 1976 there were six hundred schools on this plan nationwide, and it has remained the most popular plan nationwide (Howell). The 45-15 plan, as well as other schedules (60-20, 60-15, 90-30, trimester, quarter, quinmester, Concept 6, five track-five term, and flexible all-year) can be used with single track or multitrack plans.

The concept of year-round schooling is being looked at seriously as an alternative to the traditional schedule.

A single track plan is often used when there is no enrollment problem, but a school wishes to enhance performance. In this plan, all students follow the same schedule. A multitrack plan, by contrast, is used specifically to address school overcrowding. In this plan students are divided into groups which then overlap in their schooling, leaving a portion (often $^2/_3$–$^3/_4$) of the students in the facilities at any given time.

Currently there are more than 1.4 million students in 366 districts in 32 states involved in year-round schooling, and the number is rapidly increasing (Harp).

YEAR-ROUND SCHOOLING IN THE PACIFIC
In the Pacific Region, as well as many other places, the concept of year-round schooling is being looked at seriously as an alternative to the traditional schedule, a schedule based solely on an agricultural model and sorely out of date. No longer do students need the summers off to help plant and harvest crops. It is the feeling of many educators that year-round education better fits the requirements of the information age.

Pacific history with year-round schooling began six years ago with Waihe'e Elementary on Maui. Since then, several other public schools (Kilohana on Molokai, and Palau High School and Meyuns Elementary School, both of Palau), and three private schools (Star of the Sea, Cathedral, and Trinity Lutheran) have adopted year-round programs. Several other Hawaii schools (Ha'aheo, Ka'ewai, Helemano, Maunaloa, and Kahuku) are planning to begin year-round schooling during the summer of 1994. In addition, there are at least fifty Hawaii public schools, as well as schools in Guam and the CNMI, that are actively researching and considering the idea.

YEAR-ROUND SCHOOLING AT STAR OF THE SEA SCHOOL

Darla DeVille freely admits that she pushed Star of the Sea into year-round schooling by influencing the teachers and school board to accept the idea. In retrospect, she wishes she'd brought the community in on the planning stages, but at the time she felt an urgent need to act quickly. In Hawaii public schools, with School/Community-Based Management in place, the entire school community would organically be involved in such decisions from the beginning.

Star of the Sea devised their own innovative hybrid of the 45-15 plan to best meet the needs of their school community. Their plan divides the year into four nine-week terms, separated by three two-week vacation or intercession periods. The 45-10 plan, a "gentler" plan than the 45-15, leaves six weeks in the summer for summer school or a longer vacation period (Star of the Sea brochure). Regular school is in session 180 days a year, the same as traditional school. With intercession and summer school classes, the total possible number of school days is 228.

> The transition from a traditional schedule to year-round schooling is not easy.

The transition from a traditional schedule to year-round schooling is not easy. "It requires more work from everyone, more commitment," says Barbara McInerney, office secretary, "but the initial break is the most difficult, since it requires new methods and systems to replace the old way of doing business."

Intercession classes impact support staff by increasing work flow, particularly with regard to the organization, registration, and accounting required by intercession classes. But it is that very work and commitment that gives the school community a sense of ownership and pride in their school. And appropriate pay raises are certainly a warranted option. "In spite of the difficulty, we have not lost a teacher. We did have two families leave the school, but both returned the following fall and brought friends into the school with them," says Darla.

TEST SCORES

A commonly asked question is: Does year-round schooling increase test scores? A 1991 San Diego study showed, reading, language and math scores in year-round elementary schools improved more than those in traditional schools (Alcorn). While this is an important question, to Darla it is not the priority. "If we can create an exciting, enthusiastic learning environment with year-round schooling, I feel we have done our job."

In fact, although there has been no study of test scores per se at Star of the Sea, there is other evidence that year-round schooling has influenced learning. Since breaks are not as long, there is less time for students to forget what they have learned, and retention is better. This is empirically demonstrable by the amount of material covered each year, which has increased. Considerably less time is needed on review, and there is the chance to place students in remedial or enrichment classes every intercession, rather than having to wait until summer school, which yields a more consistent flow of learning. A continuous schedule promotes continuous achievement and challenges for gifted and talented, disadvantaged, migrant, and limited- or non-English speaking students (Hawkins). Many resources report that with frequent breaks there is less student and teacher fatigue. Joe Scrofani, a teacher at Star of the Sea, says, "For kids, this is education as it should be."

> A continuous schedule promotes continuous achievement and challenges.

In addition to the academic gain, there is also a social gain. "Kids forget how to act in school over summer break. They need to review social interactions the same way they review academic lessons," says Darla. Year-round school makes for a more continuous flow. There is less forgotten and hence less time spent playing catch-up.

INTERCESSIONS

"The school calendar is a calendar of possibilities," Darla says. "The calendar opens doors." Intercessions at schools that have gone to year-round calendars have become a time to explore some of the possibilities of the school structure, in addition to making extremely good use of the facilities.

Star of the Sea offers an array of intercession options, featuring morning, afternoon, and full-day classes that last one or two weeks. Intercession classes are often based on themes, and are often used as a way of involving community members in the school by offering them a chance to teach electives such as Hawaiiana, gardening, arts and crafts, and alternative sports, such as surfing and rock climbing. Subject experts, including university professors and members of the business community, have taught accelerated and enrichment classes, directed career exploration, or led field trips. Remedial classes in all subject areas are standard, and offer the student who has fallen behind the chance to catch up immediately, without waiting for summer school. The classes are less formal, more hands-on, and more related to "real life" than traditional school, providing a model of education that is fun, connected, and exciting. And there is always the option of just kicking back and taking a well-deserved rest or vacation.

> The alternative schedule of year-round schools can create problems for parents in the areas of child care and traditional summer plans .

SOME DRAWBACKS TO YEAR-ROUND SCHOOLING

While problems due to year-round schooling are relatively rare at Star of the Sea, they do exist. The alternative schedule of year-round schools can create problems for parents in the areas of child care and traditional summer plans. As one parent, who has additional children in other schools, commented, "It is difficult to adjust schedules to fit both sets of children."

Star of the Sea has attempted to minimize these problems by their commitment and responsiveness to the needs of parents and children. The school is open eleven hours a day, even during intercession. The cafeteria opens at 6:30 a.m. and after-school care continues to 5:30 p.m. Daily enrichment classes are offered from 3:00 to 4:00 p.m. The school has granted leaves to both students and teachers who simply couldn't resolve problems any other way.

Another concern comes from teachers who wish to take university classes or workshops during the summer. While this can be a problem, Star of the Sea has allowed teachers the time off if they need it. Their six week summer break also coincides with the university's first summer session. As year-round schooling gains additional momentum, university and other class schedules will eventually become more responsive. For schools considering the change, it is important to be flexible and provide support for students or teachers who might find themselves in unique situations.

OTHER PARENT FEEDBACK

Parents at Star of the Sea have given overwhelmingly positive response to year-round schooling. Teachers, parents, and students all comment on how kids get bored during long summer vacations, and how the shorter summer break has helped stimulate children's curiosity toward learning. "My kids are excited to return to school," one parent commented. "A six week break is long enough. Any more than that and they get bored." Another parent, who child is asthmatic and missed a lot of school, said that for the first time, thanks to the intercession remedial classes, her child is staying caught up and above average. The results of national surveys of parents who currently have children in YRE (year-round education) have shown that the majority of these parents support YRE (Hawkins).

In addition to the obvious academic benefits, many parents view the additional seasonal travel options positively.

In addition to the obvious academic benefits, and the opportunities that intercession offers, many parents view the additional seasonal travel options positively. No more do they need to take vacations only in the summer months, or face the consequence of pulling their children out of school for a spring or autumn adventure. And yet others were excited about the opportunities to teach intercession classes, and thus become involved and add something to their children's school.

Overall, the opinion is that year-round schooling is a growing trend, and that as more schools adopt the model, many of the logistical problems that exist today will be ameliorated.

CONCLUSION

Year-round schooling may seem very foreign to our calendar model of education. Yet just because something has been with us for hundreds of years doesn't mean we should continue to use it. The conditions of our lives have never changed more rapidly than they are changing now, and one of the necessary conditions of our time is flexibility and adaptability. Critical perception involves knowing when an existing paradigm is no longer useful. This seems to be the case with traditional school calendars.

The fact that Star of the Sea is a private school certainly allowed it greater flexibility to adopt year-round schooling quickly, however this situation is changing. With the advent of School/Community-Based Management and lump-sum budgeting, both of which return school control to the local level, many Pacific public schools will also have the flexibility required to make rapid changes. It seems there is no better time to begin exploring what year-rounded education can do for your school.

BIBLIOGRAPHY

Alcorn, R. D. (1992). Test scores: Can year-round school raise them? *Thrust for Educational Leadership, 21* (6), 12–15.

Harp, L. (1994, January 19). Enrollment in year-round schools is up again. *Education Week,* p. 6

Hawkins, S. (1992). *From parents to parent: A look at year-round education.* San Diego: National Association for Year-Round Education.

Howell, V. T. (1988). *An examination of year-round education: Pros and cons that challenge schooling in America.* Clarksville, TN.

PREL. (1992). *Information synthesis on year-round schooling.* Prepared by PREL (Pacific Region Educational Laboratory) for Hawaii District DOE, West Hawaii Schools.

Zykowski, J. L., Mitchell, D. E., Hough, D. & Gavin, S. E. (1991). *A review of year-round education research.* Riverside: California Educational Research Cooperative, University of California.

Making Year-Round Education (YRE) Work in Your District

A Nationally Recognized Single Track High School Model

by James C. Bradford Jr.

T he question most often asked is, why implement a year-round or extended school program? Tradition has wed school systems to the September through June school calendar for pupil attendance. However, this outmoded agrarian calendar does not provide enough time to meet the educational needs of today's children. The contemporary educational system must include programs for the at-risk, for the potential drop-out, the accelerated, the remedial, the average, and the gifted children. Year-round education addresses the needs of all children in a society which prohibits, with good reason, pupils from securing industrial employment until they are eighteen years old. A practical way to meet the educational needs of today's children in an informational, technological, and global society is to provide extended educational opportunities for learning with a year-round schedule.

In "Time for Results," published by the National Governor's Association, the following statement was made:

> It makes no sense to keep closed half a year the school buildings in which America has invested a quarter of a trillion dollars while we are under-educated and over-crowded.

Paper presented at the annual meeting of the National School Boards Association (Anaheim, California, March 22–31, 1993). © 1993 by James C. Bradford Jr. Reprinted with permission.

According to Charles Ballinger, Executive Director of National Council for Year-Round Education, "the idea of modifying the school calendars has much going for it to reduce learning loss and encourage the remediation or enrichment of a student's work." Dennis P. Doyle and Chester Finn, Jr. in the September 1985 issue of *Principal* stated, "A longer school year could help the school reformers achieve many of their objectives including higher pay for teachers, opportunities for disadvantaged and slow-learning youngsters to catch up, enrichment programs for the gifted, and simplification of child-care problems encountered by working parents during the long summer holiday."

> Seeking ways of improving student's performance and raising academic standards is a concern of every state in this nation.

Secondary schools have something in common with the graveyards. You don't change or remove graveyards, and likewise you don't change secondary schools. In order to change the public high school we are going to have to develop a plan that restructures the curriculum to that of teaching students rather than courses. Seeking ways of improving student's performance and raising academic standards is a concern of every state in this nation. In the 1930's America made a great decision when it decided to teach every American to write his/her name. Now, Americans have a new literacy standard. This new literacy standard requires that every American must be able to read, write, and decipher and read a "blue print." This new literacy standard is a mandate from the business and corporate sectors.

A Nation at Risk addressed the reasons for educational reform by the identification of thirty-six educational issues in need of improvement. One of these issues was the need to extend the school year (Year-round Education). The extended school year can assist in providing the much needed time to enhance the quality of education and the quantity of education. The issues of saving money and of alleviating overcrowding are important, but are secondary reasons for the implementation of year-round schedules.

School districts should address the reform issues based on locally identified educational needs. Buena Vista addressed the issue from the viewpoint of what would be best for the children in an industrial community with a student population that profiles the bell curve in ability. The aspirations of the people included economic development and maintenance of a viable city that would have no future if it were not for the maintenance and the recruitment of new business and industry. The city's economy centers around ten major manufacturing plants.

RATIONALE FOR CHANGING HIGH SCHOOL ORGANIZATION

As part of the program reform movement, Virginia, like many other states, has increased the requirements for students to graduate from high school from 18 to 23 units of credit for the academic diploma. The 23 unit academic diploma requires the student to take six subjects for three of their four years of high school. These students will eagerly enroll in extended school year programs. The new academic diploma makes the extended school year an integral part of the high school program.

> Parental vacation is something that must be considered in planning year-round scheduling.

The exciting part about year-round education is that it includes courses for the average student, as well as for the gifted and the remedial students. We have a large group of students in the mid-section of the bell curve (seventy percent of our students are average).

In 1972–73, report cards were being issued to the students every nine weeks. The parents were excited about the quarter system issuing the report cards every six weeks.

The governance of American education is decentralized and no one person makes the final decision on matters of education. Many of us know everything about education; "How many of us are capable of writing a first grade speller?" Norma Brekke, past president of the National Association for Year-Round Education, stated that there are two hundred forty-seven days in a school year available for instructional purposes. It is easy to divide the school year into four sixty-day blocks of time. Parental vacation is something that must be considered in planning year-round scheduling. Consideration must be given to the fact that the parents prefer a four-season vacation schedule over the agrarian schedule.

A good way to introduce an extended school program is to begin with the word voluntary. Your plan may be in trouble if you announce the program as being mandatory. If you mandate the year-round schooling without prior planning and justification, your teachers and students are going to "rise up in arms."

Year-round education is a national issue. President George Bush chose Mr. Jefferson's home in Virginia as the place to introduce his Education Agenda. One of his initiatives includes voluntary extended school programs in every school district in America. Every school district is different and you cannot take one district's program and place it in another district because of this diversity. The educational needs of adjoining districts usually vary for many reasons. Buena Vista has an industrial population with a diversified student population in need of programs for promotion, remediation, enrichment and acceleration.

> A good way to introduce an extended school program is to begin with the word voluntary.

A number of the Buena Vista patrons had expressed interest in year-round schooling for its pupils in Buena Vista. By survey, a needs assessment revealed that twenty-three percent of pupils at the secondary level would attend a voluntary extended or year-round program. The research revealed that ninety-three percent of the high school students in the city were under eighteen years of age and ineligible to work in the industrial plants, as prohibited by Virginia State Law 40.1-8. The research provided the school board with information that a large group of high school students were eligible and would attend a year-round school program. Each school district has a similar group of students waiting for an extension of the school program.

The National Association for Year-Round Education is an advocate for permissive legislation by the state and federal governments that encourages year-round education. The legislation should permit each local school district to make decisions about what is best for its children in the development of year-round programs. Each level of government must work together because we are America's Educational Team, and that is the only way year-round education will succeed. Buena Vista's extended school program has three quarters totaling 150 hours of instruction. The regular year has 180 hours of instruction. The extended school year does not have the interruption of clubs, ball games, and so forth. In 1969 we had 3% of our children enrolled in the traditional semester summer program. In 1973, the state board of education, school board, faculty, and students approved the four quarter voluntary extended school year for our high school. In the first year of operation we exceeded the enrollment goal of twenty-five percent of the regular day school pu-

Each level of government must work together because that is the only way year-round education will succeed.

pils. The extended (quarter) program has enrolled forty-seven percent to sixty-three percent of our regular high school students over the twenty-year period that the program has been in existence. The staff presented a radio program and was asked, "Would we reach eighty percent attendance in the extended school year?" Our response was, "We did not think so." In 1990, each Virginia division superintendent was given the authority to mandate year-round schooling for all children that fell below the twenty-fifth percentile. Buena Vista enacted the requirement without parental complaint.

CONSIDERATION OF SYSTEMS FOR OPERATION
Many systems of operation were considered before the establishment of an "extended school calendar" or "year-round" program for the children in Buena Vista. Three extended school year plans were reviewed in depth with the idea that each such program was not an end in itself but a vehicle for the attainment of "educational excellence" in the local school division. The extended school year plans studied extensively were the Forty-Five Fifteen Plan, the Atlanta Plan, and the Continuous Progress Plan. After much study and evaluation, the administration and staff concluded that a quarter system, with a voluntary summer quarter that included free tuition and transportation, would meet the needs of the students in grades nine through twelve.

Parry McCluer High School, located in an industrial city with a population of 7,000, has approximately 350 students in grades nine through twelve. The school has twenty-seven teachers with a pupil-teacher ration of 14.1 to 1. Fifty percent of the teachers hold advanced degrees including a foreign language and science teacher with doctoral degrees. The school is fully accredited by the Virginia State Department of Education and the Southern Association of Colleges and Schools.

ENDORSEMENTS AND APPROVALS FOR CHANGE
Before implementing the extended school year (quarter system), a number of approvals had to be obtained to insure the success of the program including:
1. Parry McCluer High School Faculty—April 1973
2. Parry McCluer High School Students—May 1973
3. Public Hearings for Citizen Input—April–June 1973
4. Buena Vista City School Board—May 1973
5. Virginia State Board of Education—July 1973

The Buena Vista City School Board in regular session on May 21, 1973, approved, on recommendation of the administration, faculty, and students, the following resolution concerning a four-quarter program of instruction in grades nine through twelve to be effective with the 1973–74 session:

> While the School Board is not approving a mandatory twelve month school plan and no child will be required to attend summer school under the compulsory attendance law, the school board approves the division of the regular school session into three parts and the change in curriculum to allow one-third credit for each completed quarter. It also approves the expansion of the elective courses in the summer and regular session and directs the administration to apply for approval from the State Board of Education for the one-third credit.

The Virginia State Board of Education in its regular meeting on March 29, 1973, approved the request of the City School Board of Buena Vista to offer unit credit in increments of less than one-half units, stating the following:

> It is understood that this waiver of current accrediting standard will allow you to organize your program at Parry McCluer High School into a quarter program which will eventually lead to a year-round operation. It is further understood that all other re-

quirements would be met, including the number of units required for graduation and the 150 clock hours of instruction.

PROGRAM OBJECTIVES

The objectives of the program were to implement a plan for the
development and implementation of a quarter plan to provide
year-round schooling in grades nine through twelve in the city
of Buena Vista. Specifically, the objectives were as follows:

1. To develop and implement a four-quarter system for
high school pupils.

2. To increase the utilization of school facilities.

3. To provide an optional fourth quarter to enable pupils
to enroll on a voluntary basis for promotion, remediation, enrichment and acceleration.

4. To provide a meaningful summer program for students
below the legal age to work in the local industries.

5. To increase students' achievement scores to a level that
equals or exceeds their abilities and/or the national average.

6. To decrease the drop-out rate to a level below the state
average.

7. To determine the success of the extended school year
(218 days) plan based on the attitude of the pupils and teachers
participating in the four-quarter system as revealed by
questionnaire.

PROGRAM CHANGE

The regular school year was divided into three sixty-day quarters. Each student is given the course objectives at the beginning
of each quarter for the quarter's academic expectations. Teachers prepared curriculum guides for each course of study with
the support of the Virginia Department of Education Pilot
Funds in the amount of $16,506.15 and a transportation grant
of $4,329.00. Report cards are sent to parents each six weeks.
Two six-week periods constitute one quarter of work and one-
third unit of credit. The pupil's final grade is determined by
weighing each six weeks grade (two-fifths or forty percent) and
the final examination (one-fifth or twenty percent). Each quarter course is an independent unit; however, courses are presented in sequence with three quarters equaling one unit of
credit.

The summer quarter offers six quarters of academic study for enrichment, acceleration, promotion and remediation. Student and faculty participation in the extended school fourth quarter is voluntary.

MONETARY CONSIDERATIONS

The superintendent of the Buena Vista City Public Schools believes that every secondary school in America should have the opportunity to develop and implement an extended year-round school program. Many of the cost considerations for an extended school year are already in the division budget, such as debt service, insurance, hospitalization, guidance, administration, textbooks, custodial services and capital outlay for busing. The three most expensive components in the implementation of an extended school year program are instructional salaries, air conditioning, and student materials.

> Every secondary school in America should have the opportunity to develop and implement an extended year-round school program.

FINANCIAL SAVINGS TO THE TAXPAYER

The financial saving to the taxpayer can be demonstrated by the cost of the extended school year as compared to the cost of a full year's instruction when a student fails a grade and has to remain in high school for an extra year. In the summer of 1992 the added instructional costs for each pupil attending the extended school year was $229.03 per pupil including transportation. The per student cost for the regular school year in 1991–92 was $4,827.75. Therefore, each student attending and advancing in the extended year program rather than repeating failed grades saved the taxpayer $4,598.92. In 1992 seven students who failed in the regular sessions elected to attend and advance in the summer session at a cost of $229.03 each per student rather than repeat at a cost of $4,827.75 each. This was a gross savings to the taxpayer of $32,191.04. The high school principal, Mr. Wayne D. Flint, firmly states that without the extended school year the administration would have to add three additional faculty members to the high school staff for an approximate cost of $120,000.00.

The school board, administration and faculty had to make provisions for the following organizational changes:

1. The teaching calendar had to be revised to conform to a four-quarter system with mini-breaks for the faculty, students and parents that conformed with community customs.

Business and industry favor year-round education for economic reasons.

2. The faculties and principal had to revise the student report cards to conform to a four-quarter system with six-week grading periods.

3. The guidance counselors and principal had to revise the student scholastic records to conform with the extended four-quarter system and six-week grading periods.

4. The curriculum in each subject area had to be revised to include expected student performances, objectives, and terminal outcomes to conform to the four-quarter system.

PROGRAM REVIEW AND EVALUATION

When the school buildings are being used on a year-round basis, you get a more favorable response when asking for community support. The citizens respond with the statement, "Oh, you're year-round; that's wonderful." Business and industry favor year-round education for economic reasons. In America, we have over one-third of a trillion dollars worth of school buildings sitting vacant twenty-five percent of the time. And yet we have the child at risk, the need for the gifted, the need for the average child, the drop-out problem, and the business' need for skilled workers who can demonstrate proficiency in reading, writing, and mathematics. About fifty percent of the Buena Vista students attend the summer quarter for promotion and remediation, and about fifty percent attend for enrichment and acceleration. In the traditional summer program three percent of the students were enrolled for remediation. You can continue the old agrarian model for scheduling the school calendar, but let's concede that it is outdated.

Buena Vista has about fifty percent of its juniors and seniors enrolled in the dual enrollment courses with students taking both high school and college courses. We have a relationship with Dabney S. Lancaster Community College that allows the high school students to take college courses taught by qualified Buena Vista teachers and to receive credit at the high school and college

Our standardized test scores have improved since implementation of the extended school year.

level. These children can and do earn up to one year of college credit while in high school. The dual enrollment tuition is paid by the school board. The teachers are employed by the college and by the school board as regular faculty members. The dual enrollment includes year-round classes. The dual enrollment program permits students to bridge the gap between high school and college. The students remain in their academic classes Tuesdays and Thursdays for additional help, and attend class on campus Monday, Wednesday, and Friday. All classes meet the standards of the Southern Association of Colleges and Schools. The research from a dissertation study by a doctoral student at the University of Rochester revealed that "all groups (parents, students, and teachers) concur that those who have attended the extended school year program have increased their knowledge more than they would have if they had not attended."[1] Our elected and governing officials think this program is one of the best programs we have implemented to improve the high school curriculum.

Regarding student age, eighty or ninety percent of the children in a school system are under eighteen years of age and are ineligible to work in most industries and businesses. Some students work to earn money for college; however, most do not. Therefore, you have a ready market to extend the school year.

Our standardized test scores have improved since implementation of the extended school year. I am not an advocate of National Standardized Test Scores, but each school official has had little choice but to deal with the issue.

Will teachers support institutionalization of extended year? Ninety-two percent of our faculty do not want the extended school program removed from the community; eighty-eight percent of our students do not want it removed. We had an independent survey that states that ninety percent of our citizens feel that we have a successful educational program.

In 1987, the Buena Vista City School Board conducted a ten-year evaluation of the four-quarter extended school year plan that brought year-round education to the high school pupils in the city of Buena Vista. The evaluation of the tuition-free, four-quarter system with voluntary enrollment for the extended school year (218 days in high school grades 9–12) revealed:

1. An effective four-quarter plan for one hundred percent of the high school pupils that included a voluntary, tuition-free fourth-quarter with over fifty-four percent of the regular day pupils enrolling during the summer quarter of 1986.

2. An increase in room or facility utilization.

3. An increase in pupil attendance with the implementation of a voluntary fourth quarter for promotion, remediation, enrichment and acceleration; nineteen percent of the pupils for promotion, forty-one percent for enrichment, thirty-nine percent for remediation, and one percent for acceleration during the summer of 1989.

4. An increase in pupil attendance during the fourth quarter for pupils below the legal age to work in local industries.

5. An increase in the pupil SRA achievement scores to a level equal to or above the national average.

6. A decrease in the local pupil dropout rate to 2.8 percent as compared to the state average of 3.3 percent (1992).

7. A ninety-two percent recommendation from the regular school faculty and an eighty-eight percent recommendation from the regular day students participating in the extended school year plan in 1986–87 for continuation of the four-quarter system in Buena Vista.

In conclusion, the follow-up studies of the extended school year at the high school level (9–12) reveal that over fifty percent of our high school students attend year-round. The reasons for attending the year-round program are promotion, enrichment, acceleration and remediation. As a result of the year-round program the student achievement scores have increased to a level equal to or greater than the national average, there has been a financial savings to the taxpayers, and there has been a decline in the drop-out rate with the exception of two years. A majority of the faculty and students report that the extended school year has not affected student extracurricular activities or interfered with family vacations.

The Buena Vista Extended School Year Plan that provides twelve-month schooling has the potential for replication on a nationwide basis. Dr. Charles Ballinger has stated the Buena Vista Extended School Year Plan is "a high school model for the nation." Buena Vista has the only operational high school in Virginia with a four-quarter plan. As stated by Ernest Boyer, in *ASCD Update,* November, 1986, "The Buena Vista extended year program is a viable extended school year program where high school students can attend for three quarters and may volunteer to extend their studies, tuition free, in a fourth quarter."

The Buena Vista Extended School Year Plan has the potential for replication on a nationwide basis.

According to Boyer, the governors task force on school facilities concluded that a year-round calendar is desirable because it:

> alleviates or at least postpones the need to build new schools during periods of temporary enrollment increases. . . . Most important, educators to date have found that improved academic performance can result from a restructured calendar that shortens the vacation periods away from formal instruction.

In a regional meeting conducted for locally elected officials and school board chairman, Dr. S. John Davis, Virginia State Superintendent of Public Instruction (1988), stated that he favored local school boards having the option to mandate summer school or an extended school year for students in need of remediation. In 1988–89, the Virginia General Assembly began providing equalized state funds to extend the school year for students scoring below the twenty-five percentile on standardized achievement tests. On the national level the North Branch High School in North Branch, Minnesota, implemented the Buena Vista Program in 1987–88 with plans to expand the program each year.

The Buena Vista Program has been cited by more than twenty state and national publications such as *The Year*

Rounder, published by the National Association for Year-Round Education, September 1991, and Summer 1988; *Smart Schools Smart Kids,* Fiske, Edward B., published by Simon and Schuster, 1991, pp. 98–99; *Washington Post,* March 2, 1992; *National School Board Association School Board News,* May 28, 1991; *U.S. News and World Report,* January 13, 1993, February 19, 1990; *USA Today,* January 14, 1986, August 13, 1986, March 6, 1989, and August 28, 1991.

> The faculty and students have continued to support the continuation of the program.

In 1989, the program received the American Association of School Administrators Award for Professional/Practitioner Excellence in Research. In 1986, the program received the Virginia Polytechnic Institute and State University Excellence Education Award, and in 1983 and in 1989 the program was recognized by the Virginia Education Research Association for significant research in the field of education.

The National Education Association has adopted the following policy statement concerning summer school, extended school year and year-round education:

> The National Education Association local affiliates must participate in the design, authorization, implementation, evaluation, and continuation of the summer school, the extended school year, and year-round schools. . . . Employment in these programs must be on a voluntary basis.

The Buena Vista School Board before implementation of the extended school year program received approval from its faculty, students and community. The faculty and students have continued to support the continuation of the program as is evident in the five-year and ten-year follow-up studies. Community and political support has been overwhelming because of more efficient building utilization and the savings to the taxpayer. The teachers, students and parents have endorsed the program because of the increased opportunities for students to learn and enroll on a voluntary basis. The superintendent has stated that he believes that "year-round education is becoming a 'long awaited' national movement." The primary purpose of the

Buena Vista program has been to enhance and improve the quality of education. By survey in Buena Vista the research fails to support the notion that the extended school year limits student participation in student activities and has a major interference with family vacations. The superintendent has stated that "the bottom line is that the nation's children have tremendous needs that can be better addressed through year-round schooling" and "American business could not operate on a schedule with twenty-five percent of its facilities on vacation each year."

NOTE

1.   Josphine F. Farrell, Case Study of an Extended School Year Program, Ed.D. Diss. University of Rochester, Rochester, New York, 1991, p. 106.

Year-Round Schooling for Academically At-Risk Students

Outcomes and Perceptions of Participants in an Elementary Program

by Wallace D. Campbell

Year-round schooling is a scheduling option that schools consider for a variety of reasons. Many school districts adopt multi-track year-round schedules as a way to cope with rapid enrollment growth without spending the money to build additional classrooms. Others hope that year-round education will increase student achievement by avoiding the long summer vacation.

This article reports the results of a study designed to examine whether year-round schooling, as compared to a traditional school year schedule, would affect the achievement and attendance of a group of at-risk elementary students. The study compared quantitative data on test scores of selected students in a single-track year-round program with those of matched students in a traditional, nine-month program. The study also assessed the perceptions of participants in the year-round program (students, teachers, administrators, and parents), and examined whether their perceptions matched the results of the program as indicated by student test scores and other student outcome indicators.

From *ERS Spectrum,* vol. 12, no. 3, summer 1994, pp. 20–24. © 1994 by Educational Research Service. Reprinted with permission.

HISTORY OF THE DISTRICT'S YEAR-ROUND SCHOOL CALENDAR

In July 1972, in response to overcrowding, the West Carrollton City Board of Education adopted a 45-15 year-round multi-track plan for kindergarten through ninth grade on an "as needed" basis. The plan went into operation in 1973 at the district's junior high school and at Schnell Elementary School, and was in effect for eight years. Under the 45-15 plan, the student body was divided into four tracks, three of which were in session at any time. Students attended school for nine weeks (45 school days), and then had a three-week vacation (15 school days). This plan increased the number of students who could be housed in a school building by 25 percent.

By 1981, room additions to the junior high school building and a gradual decrease in enrollment brought the district to the point where the space saving provided by the 45-15 plan was no longer needed. However, some parents of elementary school students requested continuation of the calendar on a single track, and the board of education approved the extension. Schnell Elementary School continues today to provide an alternative year-round calendar for those who choose it. There are four other elementary schools in the district, all of which offer the traditional nine-month school calendar.

YEAR-ROUND AND TRADITIONAL-SCHEDULE STUDENTS INCLUDED IN THE STUDY

The 60 subjects in the quantitative portion of the study were selected from Chapter 1 students in grade two who attended the West Carrollton City School District during 1990–92. The experimental group consisted of 30 students who attended Schnell Elementary, the 45-15 single-track, year-round school, for three consecutive years (kindergarten through grade two). The control group consisted of a sample of 30 students from the four traditional elementary schools in the district, who were matched with the students in the experimental group by home school attendance area. Chapter 1 students were selected because they represented an identifiable source of the academically at-risk population. The students had been placed in the Chapter 1 programs because they scored at or below the 36th percentile on the *Gates-MacGinitie Reading Test, Form K, Level 1*, which they took in the spring of their first-grade year.

Sixty-seven percent of the Chapter 1 students received free and reduced lunches, indicating economic disadvantage. It was impossible to perfectly match the subjects for socioeconomic status because of the order of priority in matching: home school, gender, ethnicity, and socioeconomic status. However, it was assumed that home school assignment was also a form of socioeconomic status matching because students in the same home school attendance area lived in the same neighborhoods.

DATA COLLECTION
Outcomes of the Year-Round Program
Student outcomes were compared on a variety of factors. The student outcome data were collected at the end of the students' third year of year-round experience, when they had completed second grade.

Basic skills gains were measured for students in both the experimental group and the control group using the *Gates-MacGinitie Reading Test, Third Edition, Form K,* which was administered in April 1991 and 1992. At that time of year, the year-round students' number of instructional days was about equal to that of the traditional-schedule students. Other student outcome data were collected during the regular school year for both the year-round and the traditional-schedule students and reported in June 1991 and June 1992 as part of the required federal Chapter 1 performance reports. These data included: absences, promotion rate, number of library books read, and reading levels completed. Socioeconomic status of students was determined by the Chapter 1 coordinator when the federal Chapter 1 project was written during the summer preceding the initiation of the study.

Perceptions of Participants in the Year-Round Program
In addition, qualitative perception data were collected in March 1993 using student, administrator, teacher, and parent questionnaires. These questionnaires were sent to 30 students, 20 administrators, 30 teachers, and 30 parents. The questionnaires asked respondents to indicate "yes" or "no" in response to a number of questions about the year-round program (for ex-

ample, "Do year-round students have higher basic skills gains than students on a traditional schedule?"). In addition, the questionnaires included an open-ended request for comments to help determine participants' feelings about the year-round calendar.

Student questionnaires were distributed to the teachers of the year-round students in the study through the inter-school mail system. The teachers were directed to meet individually with the students to guide them through completion of the questionnaire or to use the services of a parent volunteer to do this. They could also assign the questionnaire completion as homework, suggesting that parents could assist the students in recording their responses. All three methods were used in completing the student questionnaires. The student questionnaires were returned to the researcher by the classroom teachers, either in person or through the inter-school mail.

Teacher and administrator questionnaires were also distributed through the inter-school mail system, and most were returned in the same manner over the two weeks in which the student perception data were collected. Personal phone calls and written correspondence were used to follow up and obtain questionnaires not returned by the deadline.

Parent questionnaires were sent home with the current Chapter 1 year-round students with a note from the school's Chapter 1 teacher asking parents to complete the questionnaires and return them to her via the students. The teacher offered the students an incentive for returning the questionnaire the next day. Consequently, there was a 100-percent return of parent questionnaires.

DATA ANALYSIS
Both quantitative and qualitative analyses were necessary to treat the data in this study.

Quantitative Statistical Methods
Basic skills gains, absences, number of books read, and reading levels completed by the experimental group were compared to the control group using a paired samples t-test to determine

whether or not there was a significant difference between two sample means.

Chi-square was used to compare the experimental and control groups for promotion rates. Descriptive statistics or summary statistics were used whenever possible to further clarify the statistical treatments used. The mean, median, and standard deviation were used to indicate the average score and the variability of scores for the sample.

Qualitative Analysis

A narrative analysis of the open-ended questions from the questionnaires of all groups was done to identify common themes from the various responses. All open-ended responses were recorded for each question; a descriptor was assigned to each response. The next step was to combine similar descriptors and to continually delimit them until common themes or categories emerged. These categories, along with the original responses, were given to the professionals to further delimit and/or affirm the logic of the assigned categories. The final step was to define each category and to list a few examples.

RESULTS: STUDENT OUTCOMES VS. PERCEPTIONS

The first section of this study compared the year-round at-risk students with the traditional-schedule at-risk students on the following outcome variables: basic skills gains, absences, promotion rate, number of books read, and reading levels completed. The second section analyzed the perceptions of students, administrators, teachers, and parents relating to the student outcomes. The third section was a qualitative analysis of the data collected from open-ended questions on the student, administrator, teacher, and parent questionnaires.

Student Outcomes

Table 1 shows the means of the year-round and traditional-schedule students for each student outcome variable. Tests of statistical significance indicated no significant difference between the two groups of students on any of the variables. (Results of the statistical testing are found in Table 2.)

Table 1
Comparison of Student Outcomes in Year-Round School and Traditional-Schedule Schools

School Attended	Achievement Gains* (Mean)	Absences (Mean)	Promotion Rate (Mean)	Number of Books Read (Mean)	Reading Level (Mean)
Year-Round (N=30)	5.833	6.250	N/A	53.167	4.233
Traditional Schedule (N=30)	5.100	6.117	N/A	70.200	4.500

*Between April 1991 and April 1992 (end of first-grade and second-grade year) as measured by Gates-MacGinitie Reading Test, Third Edition, Form K.

Table 2
Tests of Statistical Significance: Outcomes for Year-Round Students Compared to Traditional-Schedule Students

Test	Achievement Gains Paired samples t-test	Absences Paired samples t-test	Promotion Rates Chi-square	Books Read Paired samples t-test	Reading Levels Paired samples t-test
N	30	30	30	30	30
Mean difference	0.733	0.133	NA	-17.033	-0.267
DF	29	29	1	29	29
t	.225	.102	NA	1.445	.433
Chi-square	NA	NA	0	NA	NA
Probability	.412	.460	1	.079	.334
Significance	No	No	No	No	No

N represents the paired samples. Thus, the total N of subjects is 60.
$p < .05$ for a one-tailed test.

Table 3
Perceptions of Year-Round School Participants
About the Outcomes of the Year-Round Program

	Do year-round students do better than traditional-schedule students in:									
Group	Basic Skills Yes	No	Absences Yes	No	Promotion Yes	No	Books Read Yes	No	Reading Levels Yes	No
Students	93%	7%	•		•		•		•	
Administrators	80%	20%	65%	35%	•		25%	75%	40%	60%
Teachers	50%	50%	40%	60%	33%	67%	30%	70%	•	
Parents	97%	3%	90%	10%	53%	47%	63%	37%	•	

• The wording of the questions precluded valid perceptions for these variables from administrators, teachers, and parents. Student questionnaires did not have questions pertaining to these variables.

Accuracy of Participants' Perceptions

Table 3 above shows how well the perceptions of participants in the year-round program matched the outcomes of the program for at-risk, second-grade students found by the study. It should be noted that the respondents were instructed to make a dichotomous "yes/no" choice and were not given the option to indicate a "no difference" opinion.

Both parents and students overwhelmingly believed that year-round students outperformed traditional-schedule students. The majority of administrators believed that year-round students had the advantage on basic skills gains and absence rates, but did not feel that year-round students performed significantly better than traditional-schedule students on number of books read or reading levels.

Teachers' perceptions were the closest to the actual outcomes found in the study; for all variables about which they were questioned, 50 percent or more believed that there was no significant difference between year-round students and traditional-schedule students.

Qualitative data analysis of the questionnaire's open-ended items found that year-round students were happy about attending the year-round school, and that students believed their parents, teachers, and friends also like year-round schooling. They believed that they learned more than boys and girls who did not go to school year round. Only one of the students surveyed preferred a regular school.

Administrators believed that year-round students' attitudes toward school were better than traditional student attitudes, but also said there were no fewer discipline problems for year-round compared to traditional schedule students. Administrators were undecided whether year-round administrators had a lower stress level than traditional school administrators. They saw continuity benefits for special needs students on the year-round schedule compared to the traditional schedule, and felt that there was less forgetting by year-round students at the beginning of a new school year. They believed that parents of year-round students were more supportive than traditional-schedule parents.

Teachers felt that in the year-round school they had lower stress levels than traditional schedule teachers; that continuity benefits were better for "special needs" students on the year-round schedule, and that year-round students forgot less over vacations. They felt that parental support was greater for year-round school parents.

Parents believed that school attendance was better when students attended year round, and that family vacations were easier to plan. Parents also believed that student attitude was more positive than that of traditional schedule students, and there were fewer behavior problems when students attend a year-round school. They said that participation in traditional summer activities was not a problem for students attending the year-round schedule, and that the overall quality of family life was better.

SUMMARY AND CONCLUSIONS

This study of students in one elementary year-round school provides insight into the effects of this calendar on academically at-risk students. The study was expanded to include the perceptions of students, administrators, teachers, and parents to determine whether their perceptions were consistent with actual student outcomes for the second-grade, at-risk subjects of the study. In reality, there was little consistency between the perceptions of the various groups and the actual student outcomes.

Analysis of a number of student outcomes (basic skills gains, absences, promotion rates, number of books read, and reading levels) found no significant difference in favor of the year-round students. However, students, administrators, and parents in this study generally believed that the year-round schedule produced benefits in some of these same student outcomes. When perceptions and statistically significant student outcomes were compared, teachers were more accurate in their perceptions; however, teachers did generally have positive attitudes toward the year-round schedule and felt that it had benefits for students and teachers.

The element of parental choice appears to be a factor in the success of the year-round school studied. Parents in the program seemed to be positive and enthusiastic about their children attending school all year.

The findings of this study suggest that the year-round calendar configuration may not significantly improve outcomes for all students in all circumstances. However, if the qualitative perception data are considered, it appears that the calendar configuration *can* contribute to student and parent morale, as well as decreasing teacher burnout. This information should be valuable to educational leaders in considering the potential benefits of the year-round school calendar, especially as it relates to academically at-risk students.

SELECTED SOURCES OF INFORMATION ON YEAR-ROUND SCHEDULING

Ascher, C. 1988. *Summer School, Extended School Year, and Year-Round Schooling for Disadvantaged Students.* (ERIC/CUE Digest 42). New York, NY: ERIC Clearinghouse on Urban Education. (ERIC Document Reproduction Service No. ED 298 213).

Ballinger, C. 1988. "Rethinking the School Calendar." *Educational Leadership,* Vol. 45, No. 5: 57–61.

Brekke, N. R. 1984. "Year-Round Education: Cost Saving and Educationally Effective." *ERS Spectrum,* Vol. 2, No. 3: 25–30.

Brekke, N. R. June 1991. *What YRE Can Do to Enhance Academic Achievement and to Enrich the Lives of Students that the Traditional Calendar Cannot Do.* Oxnard, CA: Oxnard School District.

Fardig, D. 1991. *Year-Round Education Program Evaluation Report of Results* (Department of Planning and Government Relations Document). Orlando, FL: Orange County Public Schools.

Herman, J. June 1988. *Phase Two Study of the Concept 6 Calendar: Do Concept 6 Schools Provide Superior, Equal, or Less Effective Educational Services for Students?* Los Angeles, CA: Research and Evaluation Branch, Los Angeles Unified School District. Publication No. 521.

Loyd, C. R. 1991. Impact of Year-Round Education on Retention of Learning and Other Aspects of the School Experience. (Doctoral dissertation, Texas A & M University). *Dissertation Abstracts International,* Vol. 52: 10-A.

National Education Association Data Search. 1987. *What Research Says About Year-Round Schools: Series 8.* Washington, DC: National Education Association Research Division.

Payne, T. April 8, 1991. *Year-Round Education and Student Achievement.* Sacramento, CA: California State Board of Education.

Peltier, G. L. 1991. "Year-Round Education: The Controversy and Research Evidence." *NASSP Bulletin,* Vol. 75, No. 356: 120–128.

Quinlan, C ., C. George, and T. Emmett. 1987. *Year-Round Education: Year-Round Opportunities.* Los Angeles, CA: California State Department of Education. (ERIC Document Reproduction Service No. 285 272).

Roby, D. E. 1992. *A Comparison of Reading and Mathematics Achievement of Students Attending a Nine Month Traditional School and a Year-Round School.* (Doctoral dissertation). Dayton, OH: The University of Dayton.

Year-Round Education: A Strategy for Overcrowded Schools

by Morton Inger

HISTORY

Confronted by overcrowded schools and tight budgets, school districts in about 30 states are keeping schools open year round. This is *not* the same as extending the school year; on a year-round schedule, students attend school the same number of days—180—as students on the traditional nine-month calendar. However, year-round education (YRE) students have several short vacations rather than one three-month summer break. By switching to the year-round calendar, districts can fit more students into existing school buildings, saving millions of dollars in construction costs.

> By switching to the year-round calendar, districts can fit more students into existing school buildings.

School districts that respond to temporary increases in enrollment by constructing new buildings run a serious risk of costly over-building, since "[l]ong after the increase in enrollment has passed, the community probably will still be paying off the bonds for the new school construction" (Alvarez, Fraser, & Durnate, 1994). Because of a growing awareness of this risk and the significant cost savings of YRE, the number of year-round schools has jumped from 287 in 1980 to more than 1,900 in 1994.

From *ERIC/CUE Digest*, no. 103, December 1994, pp. 3–4. © 1994 by ERIC Clearinghouse on Urban Education. Reprinted with permission.

SCHOOL SCHEDULING

Most year-round schools operate on a *multi-track* calendar, and group students in three or four tracks with different vacation times. While one group is on vacation, another track is using the building, thereby increasing its capacity. Thus, with a four-track calendar, a school in a building built for 750 students can serve as many as 1,000 students (Bradford, 1993).

School districts can choose from a wide selection of plans or develop their own. The most popular is 45-15, where students attend school for 45 days (nine weeks) and then take fifteen days off (three weeks).

COST-EFFECTIVENESS OF YEAR-ROUND SCHOOLS
Avoidance of Construction Costs

No matter which year-round plan is adopted, the chief reason for converting to YRE is to avoid the cost of building a new school. Expenses would be incurred for building design, engineering, construction, and furnishing, as well as for infrastructure reconstruction (streets, sewers, water, utilities, furniture). In 1987, a study done for the California State Board of Education indicated that it would cost nearly $4 million to build a 24-classroom elementary school (720 students), and more than $6 million to build a secondary school addition to accommodate 720 students (Quinlan et al., 1987, cited in Denton & Walenta, 1993).

> The chief reason for converting to YRE is to avoid the cost of building a new school.

The Oxnard (CA) Unified School District converted to year-round education in 1976. In the 1984-85 school year, its elementary enrollment increased by 644 students. If the district had been on the traditional nine-month calendar, it would have needed an additional school, at a cost of $5 million. It is believed that by converting to year-round education the district saved $16 million in new building costs over a 13-year period (Brekke, 1989, cited in Denton & Walenta, 1993).

Transition Costs

Costs for transition to the new schedule include those for feasibility studies, administrative planning time, and teacher in-service training. But these are modest compared to the avoided construction costs.

Operating Costs

A school on a year-round calendar has students in attendance for approximately 242 days each year (Brekke, 1992). Clearly, keeping a YRE school open incurs a greater overall cost than maintaining the same school for only 180 days. Maintenance, repair, and utility expenses increase; and secretaries, custodians, cafeteria personnel, nurses, counselors, bus drivers, and other staff must be available for the full 12 months, with a proportionate increase in salary. Principals' workloads increase, sometimes requiring districts to hire vice-principals to handle the increased administrative load.

> Aside from the cost savings, the primary benefit of year-round education is that it facilitates continuous learning.

However, since YRE schools are educating more students, the key financial issue is the per-pupil cost. On this standard, YRE schools have proven to be cost-effective. For example, the Pajaro Valley (CA) School District converted five schools to YRE in 1971 because it had 15 percent more students than its schools could serve on the traditional nine-month schedule. Five years later, the year-round schedule had achieved a 4.1 percent reduction in per-pupil costs (Glass, 1992). The aforementioned Oxnard District found that the operating costs of its year-round schools averaged 5.5 percent less per student than in the traditional program (Brekke, 1992).

Year-round scheduling is not the only, or the least expensive, cost-cutting option for financially strapped school districts with growing student populations. Other measures, such as double sessions or the use of temporary structures, may prove to be cheaper. These approaches, however, have educational drawbacks, while the advantages of year-round education can, in theory at least, extend beyond economics.

EDUCATIONAL BENEFITS OF YEAR-ROUND SCHOOLING

Aside from the cost savings, the primary benefit of year-round education is that it facilitates continuous learning. Students forget much of what they learned in school while on long summer vacations (Weaver, 1992). This is particularly true of disadvantaged students and those for whom English is a second language. Because students retain more when the learning process is interrupted for only short periods of time, teachers in year-round schools need to spend less time reviewing pre-vacation material.

> The shorter terms and more frequent vacations associated with year-round schooling appear to reduce dropout rates.

In addition, the shorter terms and more frequent vacations associated with year-round schooling appear to reduce dropout rates. The Jefferson County (CO) schools, for example, found that the dropout rate went from five percent to only two percent in the same schools after a year-round program was implemented. Students can miss one term and, after their personal lives are better arranged, come back to join a new class the next term.

The San Diego (CA) Unified School District compared test scores—on the Comprehensive Test of Basic Skills (TCBS) and the California Assessment Program (CAP)—from 1982 through 1990, and found significant differences in the percentage of year-round schools that maintained or improved student scores compared to the results for traditional schools (Mutchler, 1993). For example, in fifth grade, a much larger proportion of year-round schools maintained or improved TCBS reading scores than did the traditional schools, and the average improvement was significantly greater. In third grade, a much larger percent of year-round schools maintained or improved CAP reading scores than did the traditional schools, and again, the average improvement was significantly greater.

Not all results are this positive, however. Merino (1983, cited in Weaver, 1992) found no significant achievement differences between nine-month schools and those on the year-round schedule. In a study done for the California State Department of Education in 1987, year-round schools consistently scored below traditional schools with similar student populations (Quinlan et al., 1987, cited in Weaver, 1992). These results are puzzling since there appears to be nothing inherent in year-round education that could harm student achievement, and since teachers, students, and parents all feel that YRE enhances learning.

RESPONSES TO YEAR-ROUND EDUCATION
Parents
Because year-round education differs so radically from tradition, community opposition is strong at the outset. Yet parental attitudes become progressively more positive as the programs continue. For example, Cherry Creek (CO) District 5, which instituted year-round schooling in 1974, surveyed parents after the first year and found that two-thirds preferred the year-round schedule (Glass, 1992). Nationwide, other school districts have found similarly high levels of parental acceptance after the programs began.

> Like parents, teachers in year-round schools have generally positive attitudes.

The year-round schedule does, however, inconvenience families with children in both traditional and year-round schools. But parental responses are mixed: In Cherry Creek, one-third of the parents felt that year-round schooling complicated vacation planning, while one-half reported that it made vacations easier to plan (Glass, 1992).

The Riverside (CA) Unified School District surveyed parents at its seven year-round schools and found that 78 percent were satisfied with the program (Barrett, Ferrett, & Beaty, 1992). Parents felt that the shorter, more frequent vacations allowed students to remain focused and enthusiastic. Their chief concern was about the availability of child care.

Teachers
Like parents, teachers in year-round schools have generally positive attitudes, and their acceptance of the new schedule increases over time. Teachers experience few problem with the vacation times. In fact, they feel that the more frequent breaks reduce burnout and help students retain more of what they have learned. Moreover, the frequent breaks during the school year enable teachers to visit and learn from other programs and other teachers.

One concern that teachers have about YRE is that they may not be able to continue their own education—and earn pay increases—by taking university classes in the summer. But teachers have solved this problem by covering for one another at work. That is, one teacher will work during a particular break to allow another to attend summer classes.

Educators who were concerned that the year-round schedule would make accelerated learning difficult have found that the flexibility of a year-round schedule makes it relatively easy to provide accelerated classes. Many YRE schools offer between-session programs for students to participate in advanced, remedial, and enriched classes.

Students

In the Riverside survey, 82 percent of the students were satisfied with year-round schooling. They felt that the shorter, more frequent vacations reduced boredom and fatigue and helped them retain more of what they learned.

REFERENCES

Alvarez, A. Fraser, A., & Durante, R. (1994, March 21). Year-round education's impact on school districts. *Standard & Poor's Creditweek Municipal.*

Barrett, T., Ferrett, R.T., & Beaty, C. L. (1992, June). *Results of the year-round education parent, staff, and student, and student surveys.* Riverside, CA: Riverside Unified School District. (ED 358 562)

Bradford, J. C., Jr. (1993, March). *Making year-round education (YRE) work in your district: A nationally recognized single track high school model.* Paper prepared for the Annual Meeting of the National School Boards Association, Anaheim, CA. (ED 358 559)

Brekke, N. R. (1992, May). Year round schools: An efficient and effective use of resources. *School Business Affairs.*

Denton, J. J., & Walenta, B. (1993, April). *Cost analysis of year-round schools: Variables and algorithms.* College Station: Texas A&M University, College of Education. (ED 358 515)

Glass, G. V. (1992, January). *Policy considerations in conversion to year-round schools.* Tempe: Arizona State University, Tempe College of Education, Education Policy Studies Laboratory. (ED 357 476)

Mutchler, S. E. (1993, March). Year-round education. *SEDL Insights* (2). pp.1–3, 5–6. (ED 363 966)

Weaver, T. (1992, April). *Year-round education.* Portland: University of Oregon, ERIC Clearinghouse on Educational Management. (ED 342 107)

Reinventing Community by Changing the Academic Calendar: Changing Time and the Consequences

by Robin Cash, Robert D. Becker, Frank Venturo, and Paul Edwards

P **ROBLEM**
Former teachers' colleges like Western State College of Colorado often seem mired in mediocrity, tradition, and archaic ideas—our missions and curricula a product of some of the least creative and most bureaucratic agencies and organizations. We have led passive lives, following all of someone else's rules, fitting ourselves into someone else's boxes. Nevertheless, we have never lost teaching as our center and we can emerge as colleges which give large numbers of students access to liberal arts education, a tragically missing sector in public higher education. As part of the effort to achieve the status of a high quality public liberal arts and sciences institution, Western has embarked on a unique change in its academic calendar.

ABSTRACT

Western State College of Colorado is a 2600-student liberal arts and sciences college in the south-central Rocky mountains of Colorado. Western is changing its academic calendar to a 3 month-2 month-3 month-2 month year-round calendar. Western is adopting this because it provides: more flexibility in

Paper presented at the National Conference on Education of the American Association for Higher Education (Washington, D.C., March 14–17, 1993).

scheduling faculty and student workloads; more opportunities for teaching/learning innovation; more opportunity for faculty development; more efficient uses of facili-

> The intent of the change is to reorient the institution from a teacher-centered to a learner-centered community.

ties. The intent of the change is to reorient the institution from a teacher-centered to a learner-centered community. Western is transforming all of its community structures (representative government, communication/information systems, etc.) and its institutional culture. Western is also transforming its curricula to address the role and mission of the college as an exemplary undergraduate public liberal arts and sciences institution. This poster presentation focuses attention on the roles and relationships that are emerging out of this major calendar change.

WESTERN SCHOLARS YEAR
The Western Scholars Year represents an innovative strategy for creating an enhanced learning community. The Year creates opportunities for learning through problem-solving, cooperative activities, and experiential education. This is a learning-centered, rather than teaching-centered, approach that calls for much more interaction among students and faculty—the professor facilitates and encourages both individualized and group study. Because students will take courses in 12- and/or 8-week terms, their weekly schedule of classes will be more intensive. Because students will take fewer subjects, they will be able to focus greater concentration on each subject they take in a given term.

Western Scholars Year is a change in the academic calendar from one based on a traditional 16-week semester to one characterized by alternating 12-week, 8-week, 12-week, and 8-week terms. The curriculum will continue to be based on the semester-hour credit. Under the new plan, regular academic courses will be scheduled over four terms of the year—Summer, Fall, Winter, and Spring. All freshmen will attend the Fall, Winter, and Spring terms. After the freshmen year, students will have the flexibility to select the terms they wish to attend. The typical selection of terms for those students planning to graduate in four years will include three terms: two 12-week terms and one 8-week term each year.

Among the many unique features of Western Scholars Year is Western Wednesday, a day offering the campus community freedom to schedule alternative activities. Western Wednesdays are designed to encourage growth in intellectual commitment and inspire students, faculty, and staff in their development as individuals and community members. Individualized study, time for reflection, cooperative learning, co-curricular activities, field trips, special presentations by visiting artists and scholars, and student-faculty research exemplify Western Wednesday's activities.

POSTER PRESENTATION
The following four posters were presented at the 1993 National Conference on Education, sponsored by the American Association for Higher Education (AAHE), held in Washington, DC, March 14–17, 1993. The conference theme, Reinventing Community, was also the theme of this presentation—Reinventing Community by Changing the Academic Calendar: Changing Time and the Consequences.

- Changing Time and the Consequences
- Changing Time Changes Curriculum
- Changing Time Changes Pedagogy: Freshman Studies
- Changing Time Changes Space

Changing Time and the Consequences
I.   Decision made by the President to change the academic calendar and institute by the next year.

II. President charges a 16-member campus-wide steering committee to facilitate and coordinate planning, decision making, and implementation, and to review and evaluate the program's success.

- Fear
- Risk
- Power
- Truth
- Enthusiasm/Excitement

- Intimidation
- Sabotage
- Intensity
- Review and Reform
- External Forces
- Internal Forces
- Communication
- Cooperation

Changing Time Changes Curriculum
Class modules designed for a variety of pedagogical approaches and outcomes
- 12-week terms
  50-minute modules meet M T TH F
  100-minute modules meet M TH or T F
- 8-week terms
  75-minute modules meet M T TH F
  150-minute modules meet M TH or T F
- Evening classes and field studies variable

Flexibility in course offerings
Traditional - Block - Cluster

Western Wednesdays: A break in the intensified schedule
- No scheduled classes before 2:00 p.m.
- Individualized study, cooperative learning, co-curricular activities, field trips, special presentations, student-faculty research
- Coordinating committee to give focus and meaning

Changing Time Changes Pedagogy: Freshman Studies
- A learning-centered first-year curriculum
- Seminars encourage development of the whole individual
- Peer, staff, faculty advising
- Student support services through evaluation and career planning
- Residential living program
- Shared learning: Faculty-student and student-student

- Cooperative classroom experiences
- Experiential learning

Changing Time Changes Space

I. The traditional calendar shaped perceptions of facility use

- Classrooms structured for presentational-style teaching
- Classrooms schedules to accommodate presentational-style teaching

II. Modify the academic calendar to rethink facility use and time

- Reconfigure classrooms for interactive-style teaching
- Schedule classes to accommodate interactive-style teaching and to encourage around-the-clock learning

Year-Round Education:
The Change Process

Society can only pursue its normal course by means of a certain progression of changes.—John Viscount Morley

T he first two sections inform the reader about year-round education and provide examples of schools that have implemented it; this closing section speaks to the process of change involved in shifting from a traditional school calendar year to a continuous school calendar year, for the decision to reexamine existing traditions is, in itself, revolutionary. In fact, speaking to the issue of change in the schools, one of the authors likens the traditional high school to a graveyard. "You don't change . . . graveyards, likewise, you don't change secondary schools," laments Bradford, in a statement that many readers will attest to. Yet the change to year-round schooling *is* possible, as indicted by the examples cited thus far in the collection. Now, in the final gathering of articles, seasoned voices speak authoritatively about the dos and don'ts of the change process for schools interested in year-round education.

Dlugosh sets the cornerstone for the initial investigation of year-round education in an enlightening discussion about quality schools and the myths of the nine-month school year. With the average number of school days in American schools at 178, the author notes pressing calls for more time to learn and different arrangements for learning. Using a case study model, the author examines ideas about time patterns and learning. In the preface, he reviews the findings, which provide no conclusive evidence that more time in school increases test scores. Logical arguments, on the other hand, do support moving away from the nine-month school year. Those arguments in favor of the year-round schedule include continuous learning patterns, better use of facilities, alleviation of overcrowding, and opportunities to extend learning experiences.

In his analysis of the feedback received from educators, parents, and students about the proposed calendar, the information has been organized into eight general categories: *intersessions* (two weeks between sessions), *interruptions* (allocating present time differently), *vacations and sports, early starting date, stress, adding days to the calendar, finance and research,* and *evaluation.*

While the proposal to switch to year-round education was not accepted by this school district, the case offers insight into the reasons for rejection and possible avenues to explore if schools are to break with "old habits." Suggestions for other school districts in the early stages of the change process include: continued education for the public about alternatives, evidence of the advantages and disadvantages, and forums for ongoing dialogue. In this comprehensive piece, Dlugosh elaborates on the aforementioned suggestions, offering great insights on the subject for the interested reader.

In the second article of the section, Greenfield offers a case for change by citing sequential phases, such as planning, adoption, implementation, and institutionalization. In this well-documented piece, the author cites an "exploratory" case of year-round education in which the motivational factors were academic and learner centered rather than financial or logistical.

Following the study, Greenfield charts information derived after a four-year study of the advantages and disadvantages of year-round education. Using the exploratory case, others contemplating this approach can follow the guidelines recommended in the closing section. As in any change effort, negotiation of the stages of change is a necessary first step. Targeting curriculum and instruction, as well as the school calendar, is a must if academic improvement is the goal. Community needs must be fully assessed to effect significant, long-lasting change.

A survey of public opinion regarding year-round education is the focus of an article by VanderHooven. Given an example of a year-round education calendar, the participants were then asked their opinion of the schedule. The results—60 percent against, 27 percent for, and 13 percent undecided— suggest that the public has a strong, and negative, view of year-round education. The study further suggests that the public may be unaware of the benefits, such as decreased drop-out rates and less "burn out" among teachers and students, an understanding of which may have resulted in more positive survey results.

A complex article by Gándara and Fish reports on a study of three schools involved in an extended school-calendar year. Employing this reform strategy, all three schools were able to demonstrate increases in academic achievement, a high level of parent/teacher satisfaction, and a cost effectiveness in regard to utilization of the facilities. Lark School, Palm Avenue School, and Brady School, all located in California, reported overall positive results, but also cited some problems that arose. Among these difficulties are the coordination effort itself, the requirement for certified staff in every class, hiring of quality staff, and space limitations. Yet the conclusions drawn from the study suggest viable avenues for change: year-round education is feasible for many communities and can open doors to many kinds of innovations; intersession programs can be an important adjunct to the regular school curriculum; year-round education can work to reduce class size; teachers can be given options to contract for different work schedules; and schools may find that experimenting with school dynamics can promote more positive attitudes in the classroom. In light of this extensive study, year-round education in general seems to be a viable strategy.

One final article completes this section on the change process involved in moving to year-round education. In a succinct piece by Knox, the reader is introduced to "seven rules" to year-round schooling, in which the author advocates research and dialogue as the keys to implementation of year-round education. Knox writes about his district's move to year-round education, telling how (in spite of the intense summer heat) they have implemented it successfully following these seven rules:

1. Do your homework
2. Involve your community
3. Form a support group
4. Encourage honest feedback
5. Develop a multi-year plan
6. Collect ongoing data
7. Remain flexible

The author concludes that, in this case, year-round education was not a solution in search of a problem, but rather a reform strategy they chose to investigate in order to increase student achievement. Recommending the seven rules, the author assures the reader of a stronger program and warns of some avoidable roadblocks to implementation.

Quality Schools and the Myth of the Nine-Month School Year

by Larry L. Dlugosh

In an international comparison of educational systems, the National Center for Education Statistics (1992) listed the average number of days in a school year for American elementary and secondary students at 178 days. Because states have the authority to establish the number of days the public schools shall be in session and because the number of student days required by each state is similar, it would be easy to conclude that it is a matter of policy in the United States for schools to meet for approximately nine months during the calendar year. Local boards of education and school administrators play a major role in determining how time in the school day and school year is arranged and in each classroom teachers have the ultimate responsibility for matching the educational program with the pieces of time allocated for instruction. At each juncture, time is the element that controls the learning environment. There is a growing consensus among educators and the public that either more learning time or different arrangements for learning time are needed if schools are to accomplish their educational and social responsibilities. New technologies, global economies, rapidly changing social environments, the changing of American life-styles, and the needs of students are driving the dialogue about time and school.

Arguments in favor of increased time in school are not new. During the past 80 years requests to examine the length of

Paper presented at the annual University of Oklahoma National Conference on Creating the Quality School (Oklahoma City, Oklahoma, March 31–April 2, 1994). © 1994 by Larry L. Dlugosh. Reprinted with permission.

the school day and school year have been numerous. The American School Board Journal (1990) cited an article from 1917 that called for increasing the amount of time students were in school. The article revealed, "an ever increasing number of superintendents is advocating a radical reduction in the length of summer vacations and is seeking a correspondingly longer school term. The success of summer sessions and the splendid results achieved from experimental "all year schools" indicates clearly that schools are overlooking an opportunity for better educational service and greater economy. From then until now the issue of reallocating student time in school has been hotly debated. Generally the subject of time in school arises when there is a crisis of confidence in the nation's ability to conduct its business or when taxpayers question the rising costs of public education. Most recently the issue of our capacity to complete economically with other developed nations, particularly Japan, raised questions about the necessity to increase the number of school days required of American students. It is somewhat of a mystery that the number of school days required of American students is linked so closely with the inability of the "big three auto makers" or other corporate entities to retain their sales dominance in the world market. It is especially intriguing since Ford, the Chrysler Corporation, and General Motors most recently made claims that they were positioned to once again dominate the world automobile market. What is curious is that from the time they lost market share to the time they have presumably regained it, the school year in America has remained virtually the same.

> Generally the subject of time in school arises when there is a crisis of confidence in the nation's ability to conduct its business.

Perhaps there are many more compelling arguments for moving to a full time school system than economic competitiveness alone. The recent wave of school restructuring has caused us to look seriously at the mission of American schools and to redefine what we, as a nation, want and expect from our public schools. Studies of extended school years and year-round education have not provided conclusive evidence that more time in school increases test scores on academic measures.

However, there are logical arguments to address the need for moving away from the nine-month on, three-month off cycle of schooling. A more continuous learning pattern, better use of school facilities, the alleviation of overcrowding in certain districts, and the opportunity to extend learning experiences are a few of the reasons to consider other configurations of the school calendar. Moorman and Ergermeier (1992) stated, "a community should base its faith in a school not on the school's conformance with a structure thought to provide predictability and control but on the strength of the school's mission and plans for achieving it."

> There are logical arguments for moving away from the nine-month on, three-month off cycle of schooling.

The purposes of this paper are to examine ideas about time patterns, learning and school and present a plan for districts to use if they are considering the adoption of alternative time patterns. A case study (Dlugosh, 1992) was used to illustrate an attempt by one school district to modify its calendar to improve instructional opportunities for student learning. With the case study as a basis, a plan was developed to assist other school districts to begin or continue the dialogue with their publics about alternatives to the nine-month school calendar.

A CASE IN POINT: MIDWESTERN COMMUNITY SCHOOLS

In 1991, a progressive school district (Midwestern Community Schools) with a K–12 population of 4700 students, long recognized for its innovative programs, high student achievement, and excellent parental support, proposed to implement a "custom calendar" that would have modified the traditional school year. The district was both financially and educationally sound and the plan it presented was aimed at improving the capacity of the district to provide additional instruction for students. The objectives of the proposed "custom calendar" and a brief explanation of the reasons for the changes are listed below.

  • *To provide for 10 additional days of instruction by the year 2000.* Explanation: increased demands of the information age and changing societal needs have increased the demands on instructional time; more time is needed to support additional instruction.

• *To create a more continuous learning program.* Explanation: Loss of learning occurs over extended breaks, especially during long summer breaks; this loss can be reduced and more learning can be retained through a continuous calendar.

• *To provide quality intersession programs.* Explanation: Intersessions, the 10 day periods separating the instructional blocks, would be used to provide for an extension of learning time for students to practice basic skills, expand their understanding in selected curriculum areas, and provide extended learning opportunities on and off campus.

• *To procure non-traditional financing and support for intersession programs.* Explanation: To extend learning opportunities without it becoming a burden on district taxpayers.

• *To reduce stress and fatigue for students and teachers.* Explanation: More frequent, shorter, and better spaced vacations offer opportunities for staff, families, and students.

The objectives reflect attention to student needs, a desire to offer quality break periods combined with the instructional advantages offered via intersessions, and an attempt to balance financial obligations among local agencies and outside funding sources. Implementation of the proposed calendar would have necessitated an August 3rd opening date for the Fall semester and would have added two days to the overall school calendar during its first year of operation.

Midwestern Community Schools planned a variety of opportunities to inform its publics about the proposed custom calendar. It conducted 28 orientation meetings, 28 follow-up meetings throughout the Fall and Winter, and 2 public hearings in the early Spring to provide parents, students, staff, and patrons of the district with information about the goals and objectives of the proposed calendar and to outline the districts' needs for changing the school calendar. Approximately 1700 people attended one or more of the sessions. Feedback about the custom calendar was recorded and transcribed. A brief analysis of the transcripts yielded information organized in eight general categories.

Intersessions

473 items related to the concept of intersessions, the two week period between each quarter. For the most part, people wanted to know more about the purpose of the intersession, the type of programs to be held during intersessions, how students would be selected to attend, how much intersessions would cost and who would pay for them.

Interruptions

Many of the participants at the orientations and hearings indicated the district should determine how interruptions during the regular calendar year could be reduced and the time used for instruction. 164 questions and comments addressed interruptions and allocating the time already available to better use.

Vacations and Sports

155 items were recorded under the category vacations and sports. Comments ranged from "vacations are important family times" and "an early start would interrupt them" to "athletic calendars would need to change to accommodate the school calendar, but they won't." Many people indicated the intersessions would provide new opportunities for family vacations.

Early Starting Date

Most of the 115 comments recorded in this category referenced the August 3 starting date as "too early" or "give us some lead time to prepare for an earlier starting date—maybe in a year or two." Generally, people were reluctant to "rush into" the earlier starting date. (The district had planned to implement the custom calendar in the upcoming school year and parents did not feel ready to accept a change that was so immediate.)

Stress

108 comments were related to the area of relieving stress on students and teachers by providing short, well timed breaks. There appeared to be an equal split between those who believed the custom calendar would relieve stress on families and those who thought it would cause more stress.

Adding Days to the Calendar
There was considerable positive agreement in 82 comments about adding days to the calendar. Generally favorable; some thought 10 days were not enough and the district should consider adding more days.

Finance
86 responses related to cost and taxes. Most people wanted much more information about the cost of the proposed calendar. They wanted definite figures and they wanted to know how costs might impact people on fixed incomes.

Research and Evaluation
47 responses indicated a need for more research about the effects of extended school years and how the impact on students and achievement would be evaluated. Generally, they wanted to be assured of the benefits they were likely to accrue as a result of any change.

The people who spoke at orientation sessions and hearings indicated a need for more information about the new plan and requested time to study the issue. Some were very opposed to any tinkering with the present school calendar, but most indicated support to investigate the issue further. Almost 400 people attended the school board meeting where the issue was scheduled for a vote. They asked the board to delay implementation of the custom calendar and to investigate how the district could take better advantage of the current time pattern through the elimination of interruptions to the learning process.

After reviewing testimony from people in attendance at the public hearings and listening to parents and patrons at the board meeting, the board of education decided to delay full implementation of the custom calendar and take the advice of the patrons to study current allocations of time in the schools to try to determine if additional instructional time could be gained by eliminating some of the interruptions to the school day.

Midwestern Community Schools began its time-utilization study with teachers at the elementary school level. After surveying the elementary faculty district officials reported the following findings to the board and administrative staff:

• Approximately 67% of the teachers said they preferred to devote between 4.5 and 5 hours to student learning activities. 73% of the teachers indicated they actually devoted between 4 and 5.5 hours of time to student learning activities during their present calendar day arrangement.

• 78% of the elementary teachers indicated the length of the school day was just right, 17% said it was too short and 5% said it was too long.

• 70% of the teachers indicated the length of the school year was just right, 17% thought it was too short and 13% believed it was too long.

• Over 62% of the elementary teachers surveyed estimated they could possibly gain 15 minutes, but less than 30 minutes of instructional time per day by reducing interruptions such as pulling students out of class for band, P.E., and resource room and by the district['s] providing them with additional help to work with learning disabled students.

• 61% of the elementary teachers indicated they could make better use of existing instructional time by integrating content areas within the curriculum. Well over half of the teachers surveyed said instructional time could be enhanced by providing them with uninterrupted planning time (90%), providing teacher aides and other support staff to assist teachers (61%), and scheduling activities such as band and strings before or after the regular school day (56%).

> Teacher support for extending the number of school days or lengthening the school year was not evident at the elementary level.

Teacher support for extending the number of school days or lengthening the school year was not evident at the elementary level. The same was found to be true in an independent study of the secondary school staff, although many of the secondary teachers indicated they would appreciate an opportunity to be employed on an 11 or 12 month basis.

The case study serves as one example of the frustration facing educators who feel pressured to complete their mission under current time constraints while the world around them is exploding with new information and change, but are not able to shift the organization toward a new pattern of thought. It also offers insights about school and time as viewed from the per-spective of parents and other taxpayers. In that sense, it pro-vides an opportunity for schools to create a dialogue about the need to reassess priorities related to time and learning. There were probably many reasons for the reluctance of people in Midwestern Community Schools to reject the custom calendar; in this paper we can only speculate as to why the issue was not accepted on its face.

• First, the dialogue about the custom calendar with the clients of the school district took place after the proposal was developed, even though it was developed with the assistance of citizens representatives from across the district. The school may have assumed that their reasons for requesting additional in-structional time was a widely shared notion.

• Second, it is difficult to convince parents and other dis-trict patrons that additional time deserves their support when a majority of the teaching staff was not favorably inclined to sup-port extensions of the day or year.

• Third, students in the district were already achieving at high levels as measured by traditional tests, so there was no evi-dence of any type of educational crisis. By the same token, par-ents were satisfied with the achievement level of their children so they saw little need to bolster the instructional delivery system.

• Fourth, many of the patrons and parents of the district had the means to provide additional educational experiences for their children as they saw fit. Some of them used the sum-mer months for such experiences as academic camps, foreign travel, and extended family vacations.

• Fifth, perhaps not enough evidence was brought forward to convince people that 10 additional days per school year pro-vided additional academic advantages for students.

• Sixth, change is difficult. Shifting from a traditional school calendar to a new concept of time creates uncertainty on the part of the staff and patrons. It is complicated by the fact that many people are not aware of the variety of ways in which a school can allocate time. Most people have only heard about lengthening the day or year.

The situation reveals the power of the traditional mental model of school and time in the United States. It also serves to remind educators that they will need to present evidence to counter old arguments about time in school and to present logical and compelling reasons about the benefits to be gained from modifying the traditional school calendar. The good news is, there appears to be a growing body of evidence to suggest the alternative school calendars are gaining acceptance. The not-so-good news is old habits are difficult to break.

> The situation reveals the power of the traditional mental model of school and time in the United States.

THE DIFFICULT TASK OF CHANGING MENTAL MODELS

"Metanoia" is the Greek word Senge (1990, pp. 13–14) used to remind us that the deeper meaning of "learning" involves a fundamental shift of mind. "Real learning," he said, "gets to heart of what it means to be human. Through learning we perceive our world and our relationship to it. Through learning we extend our capacity to create, to be a part of the generative process of life." While there may be plenty of evidence available to help people shift their mind in the direction of alternative time patterns for school, it will not be easy because there is a certain comfort level with the traditional school year. Bisesi (1983) wrote about the tendency of people to become comfortable with the way things are, especially in the face of the introduction of alternative prospects or methodologies. He described this level of comfort as frozen evaluation. "Once we have found cozy niches for people, organizations or societies," he stated, "we fix those descriptions in our minds as immutable reference points." The American school year appears to be one of those immutable reference points. Regardless of the difficulty, changes do occur. Schein (1969) described change as a three level process; *unfreezing, changing, and refreezing.* During the unfreezing stage, Schein said, "individuals who will be responsible for implementing the change and those directly affected by it must be convinced of the need for change. It is a time of letting go of old beliefs and patterns and developing a desire to try the new. Stage two, implementation of the actual change, requires the development of new patterns of behavior based on new information. The third stage, refreezing, involves the stabilizing and general acceptance of the change."

Assuming the Midwestern Community Schools were in the first stage of the change process described by Schein, attempting to convince the general public that a need for change existed, it was necessary to provide some suggestions to assist them to move through the entire process. The suggestions are as follows:

1. Continue to provide an education for the community about the alternatives available for scheduling learning time for students.

2. Offer evidence about the advantages and disadvantages of the alternative time patterns and their impact on student achievement and student attitude.

3. Establish a forum for a dialogue about the function and purpose (mission) of school in a post-industrial society; a society where production time is measured in fractions of seconds rather than days, months, or years.

EDUCATE ABOUT ALTERNATIVE TIME PATTERNS AVAILABLE TO SCHOOLS

Because the traditional time frame for schools is comfortable and people are not well acquainted with alternative models, it is necessary to provide as much information as possible about the efforts to reframe time in school. Since April of 1992, the National Education Commission on Time and Learning has been studying "the quality and the adequacy of the time U.S. students devote to learning" (Anderson, 1994). Among other things, they have looked at the amount of time allocated to learning activities, the way children use time outside of school, the length of school days and school years and the political and financial issues related to time and schooling. The results of their study will be useful in helping people define some of the alternatives to the traditional school day and school year. Some of the alternative patterns are:

• *The Extended Day:* The extended school day generally refers to a longer school day and/or a day that includes before- and after-school programs.

• *The Extended Year:* Schools that are in session for 200 days per year or longer. The extended year option provides an opportunity for students to attend for 11 months and complete 12 years of instruction in 10 years. Anderson (1994) reported only 10 schools offering extended learning programs of 210 days or more when the Commission on Time and Learning began their study in 1992, but stated more schools were beginning to experiment with the idea.

• *Year-Round Schools:* The term, year-round schools, generally describe a pattern whereby the 180 days of student time is redistributed in alternative time tracks. Peltier (1991) discussed year-round schooling as a means of providing options for students and families. He describes two types of year-round schedules: "single track and multi-track." Each plan offers students options for when they will be in attendance and when they will be on vacation. The single track is a variation of the traditional school calendar in which all students attend school at the same time and vacation at the same time even though their school year may be designed in a 45 days of class and 15 days of vacation plan. Multi-track plans offer the 45-15, 60-20, 60-15, 90-30, trimester, quarter, and quinmester options and have students on various track at various times. Students must attend three quarters, two trimesters of four quinmesters and they can select their "off time" according to their needs. They also have the option of attending classes during their "off time" to enhance or accelerate their learning.

• *The Reorganized Day:* The reorganized school day is based on the idea that the typical, finite, tightly scheduled class periods do not necessarily [work] for every learning activity. The reorganized day takes into consideration the length of learning experience based on student need. The Copernican plan is an example of the reorganization of learning experiences based on curriculum demands and student need (Carroll, 1994). This plan exemplifies the "shift of mind" Senge (1990) talked about; it challenges the traditional organizational pattern of class periods.

The serious investigation and innovation of alternative time patterns appears to have gained impetus as a result of issues raised in the 1983 report, *A Nation at Risk,* The National Goals of Education, and the growing concern over the capacity of public schools to provide an appropriate education for America's youth.

RESEARCH ABOUT ALTERNATIVE TIME PLANS

Schools do not and should not adopt the simplistic notion that there are only two ways to increase student productivity in schools: longer days or longer years. "What is key," according to Moorman and Ergermeier (1992), "is that schools be able to adopt clear and persuasive missions sufficient to distinguish them in meaningful ways from other alternatives, that they implement programs that concentrate resources and effort toward achievement of their missions, and that they are able to learn systematically from their own experience and continue to make corrections for shortcomings in their performance." Traditional time patterns may be one obstacle to learning that is in need of correction. As discussed earlier, there are a number of options from which schools can develop alternative time patterns. Many logical arguments, ranging from better utilization of school facilities to increased learning opportunities for students, have been advanced during the past few years. A Harvard University research team found the Copernican schedule (reorganized day) enabled students to complete high school courses on a very intense schedule and do significantly better than their 180 day counterparts (Carroll, 1994). Glines (1987) reported year-round educational programs "help people individually, and society in general, by providing calendar, curriculum, and family options which more closely fit the changing lifestyles, work patterns, and community involvements for large segments of the population." According to Toch (1993), "In a 1991 review of 100 research projects, Herbert Walberg of the University of Illinois at Chicago found that in 9 out of 10 instances student achievement rises with the amount of time in class."

While the proponents of alternative time patterns can speak to easing overcrowded conditions and providing options for families and students a number of flags have been raised about the notion of merely increasing time without a corre-

> There are a number of options from which schools can develop alternative time patterns.

sponding increase in school quality. In reference to the issue of time and the quality of schools, Boyer (1983) said, "many school people seem more concerned about how long students stay in school than what they should know when they depart. . . . More substance, not more time is our urgent concern!" In *A Place Called School,* Goodlad (1984) suggested, "If our interest is in quality educational experiences, we must stop providing only time. I would always choose fewer hours well used over more hours en-gaged in sterile activities. Increasing the

> "Increasing the amount of instruc-tional time does not guarantee an increase in engaged time— time spent actively engaged in learning."

days and hours in school settings will in fact be counterproduc-tive unless there is a simultaneously marked improvement in how time is used" (p. 283). Berliner and Fisher (1985) added their doubts about increasing quantity of time without enhanc-ing the skills and knowledge of teachers. Hossler (1988) report-ed, "research generally supports the conclusion that increased instructional time has modest positive effects on learning. How-ever, the relationship between time and achievement is not strong, and policy-makers should not expect large gains to re-sult from increasing the amount of instructional time in the school day/year. Moreover, increasing the amount of instruc-tional time does not guarantee an increase in engaged time— time spent actively engaged in learning." Her claims were sub-stantiated earlier by Walberg (1982) and Karweit (1984) and others.

While the concern about the legitimate use of additional student time remains as valid as it was during the early 80's, there appear to be additional forces driving the debate about the pluses and minuses of alternative time patterns. During the late 1980's and early 1990's the dialogue about restructuring intensi-fied and more schools joined with those already offering ex-tended school years. In 1992, the National Association for Year-Round Education reported 204 public school districts on year-round schedules compared to 152 in 1991. "The move is driven by education and economics," according to Charles Ballinger (1992), the Executive Secretary of the National Year-Round School Association. "More people are doubting the wisdom of long summer vacations that thwart students' educational progress and leaves valuable school facilities dormant for long periods of time," he said. States such as California and Texas have long been proponents of year-round schedules to help overcrowding from growing populations and alleviat[e] the need to build new buildings. Concern over shrinking school budgets and overcrowding have combined with changes in the U.S. social demographics. Many families are comprised of two wage earners while 14.9 million have a single parent as sole supporter. During the 1990's, 82% of women in the workforce have school-aged children (Anderson, 1994). Increased levels of violence in the society have put more children at risk than any previous time in our history. All of this has changed the perspective of Americans about the function of the school and has propelled the issue of increased time in school to a higher level of dialogue. For all of these reasons, the idea of increasing students' time in school seems to be increasingly more acceptable to the public. Michael Barrett, in the November 1990 issue of the *Atlantic Monthly*, reported 33% of Americans polled in 1959 were in favor of increasing the number of days per year spent in school but by 1989, 48% were in favor. The 25th Annual Gallup/Phi Delta Kappa Poll of the Public's Attitudes Toward the Public Schools (1993) reported 52% of the public endorsed an increase in the amount of time students spend in school by extending the school day or school year, 47% favored an extended school year, 33% favored an extended school day, and 5% preferred Saturday morning classes as a method for increasing student time.

> The idea of increasing students' time in school seems to be increasingly more acceptable to the public.

EXAMINING THE FUNCTION OF SCHOOLS IN THE 21ST CENTURY

Contemporary American society calls for a re-examination of the traditional school calendar. Contrary to popular opinion, schools have not always met for just nine months. Brekke (1992) reminds us that "prior to and through the 1800s, our urban centers, such as New York, Philadelphia, Boston, Baltimore, Chicago, and Cincinnati, maintained schools for 11 to 12

months a year in response to a burgeoning immigrant population. By 1915, largely due to the onset of the industrial revolu-
tion . . . the nine month school year became the nation's standard. The 'traditional school year' has existed in virtually the
same form for the last 75+ years."

There are plenty of reasons to suspect rapid changes in the
society have influenced the ideas about almost all services expected from some of the nations traditional institutions. For example, banks are quick to point out their expanded time
frames; with the aid of telecommunications "bankers hours"
are, at last, 24 hours a day! Medical services are available at
emergency rooms and free standing clinics at any time of the
day or night. Many businesses are open 7 days a week to accommodate customers who are at work during what used to be traditional shopping times. In addition to their expanded hours of
operation, many of these traditional institutions have taken on
additional functions. Banks, for example, offer brokerage services, insurance plans, bill paying services, social and travel opportunities, and 24 hour account access. Medical centers offer
wellness classes, health fairs, menu planning, counseling services, and a variety of specialized clinics. And when we can't get
what we want from our traditional institutions, we invent new
ones to take their place; witness the rise of United Parcel Service
and other like carriers who have out-delivered the U.S. Post Office. What would lead us to believe the public schools could or
should escape these trends?

In an address to educators gathered to celebrate the 100th
anniversary of a private, midwestern college, John Goodlad
(1994) discussed the importance of a well defined mission for
the nations elementary and secondary schools and he called on
the audience to reflect on the function of schools in contemporary society. Goodlad expressed his view that the primary function of schools is the care and shelter of the young, the provision of a safe and nurturing environment during the day.
"Child caring," he stated, "is an educational process." If, as
Goodlad suggests, the school functions as the place designated
by society to care for children during the day, it will likely serve
as the primary depository for the young until they are old
enough to fend for themselves. This function does make sense,
especially in the 1990's when dual income families and single

parent families are the majority. America's families rely on school as much or more than during anytime during recent history, but schools have been slow to warm up to the idea that they serve primarily as care providers. In the sense that schools function as child care centers, there may be little anyone should do to radically adjust the time structures associated with this function. However, the picture changes when purpose is added to function. Parents want more than custodial care; they want children to develop their intellectual and social skills in an environment that is caring and educational. That being the case, the mission of the public schools seems abundantly clear: "to create a supportive environment where children will be prepared to enter the human conversation."

> Schools have been slow to warm up to the idea that they serve primarily as care providers.

TIPS FOR SCHOOLS: ENGAGING THE COMMUNITY IN THE DIALOGUE

Excellent outcomes require excellent planning. If we are willing to give serious consideration to the "Who, What, Where, When, Why, and How" of public education in the contemporary society, it seems new mental models for school must be raised and explored. Many of the models should address the issue of providing alternative time patterns for students. The following guidelines may serve to assist school districts in the creation of a dialogue about the future of schools and schooling with the community:

• *Sponsor public forums* to inform citizens about the school's mission in contemporary society. Adopting Goodlad's ideas, the school serves as a care provider *and* delivers an important service. Schools have accepted an expanded role in child care as the needs of parents have increased; that role alone requires additional time and attention. Rapid changes in information and technology have had a tremendous impact on the economy and lifestyle of citizens and the school. It is difficult for schools to deliver their services in the time available.

– Examine how the functions and purposes of schools have been changed by other systemic changes.

• *Organize school/community learning teams* to examine the mental models we now use to frame our beliefs about schools and schooling and develop new models that are more in harmony with the lifestyles that exist today.

• *Develop a plan* to assist the school to better meet its obligations and to accomplish its mission.

– One of the objectives of the plan must be to consider alternative time patterns for schools.

– It is important to develop a plan that enables people to move at a comfortable rate toward expanded goals and new time patterns.

– Part of the plan should be to develop a process to assist the district to continuously scan the environment for trends and the needs of clients.

• *Implement the plan over time and monitor it constantly.* The plan must be flexible so changes can be made as soon as new information about variables that impact the business of the school are discovered.

• *Provide continuous feedback* to everyone concerned about the progress of the plan. Help them understand how and why adjustments were made and the impact those adjustments are likely to have on the successful accomplishment of the school mission.

– Feedback should be provided about student and teacher attitude toward school under the new time arrangements, attendance, student progress toward individual and group goals, achievement scores, etc.

The move away from traditional calendars toward alternative time patterns must be understood and accepted by the public. It is a significant move with tremendous potential. When talking about alternative time patterns for schools, Ballinger (1993) stated, "We're not just changing the school calendar, we're changing the whole rhythm of American life."

REFERENCES

Ballinger, C. (1988). "Year-round school: When you get rid of the emotional-ism—does it make sense?" *Instructor,* August 1988.

Berliner, D., and Fisher, C. W., eds. (1985). *Perspectives on instructional time.* New York: Longman, 1985.

Brekke, N. (1992). "Year-round schools: An efficient and effective use of re-sources," *School Business Affairs,* v. 58, no. 5, May 1992.

Boyer, E. (1983). *High school.* New York: Harper & Row, 1983, pp. 83–84.

Dlugosh, L. (1992). "A study of time allocations in the westside community schools," unpublished.

Glines, D. (1987). "Year-round education: A philosophy." *Thrust,* May/June 1987 (p. 14–17).

Harnischfeger, A. (1986). "Findings and recommendations regarding lengths of school day and year," in *A nation at risk: Some reflections,* unpublished.

Hossler, C., and others. (1988). "The relationship of increased instructional time to student achievement." Bloomington, IN., *Policy Bulletin: Consortium on Educational Policy Studies,* March 1988.

Karweit, N. (1988). "Time on task: The second time around," *NASSP Bulletin,* v. 72, n. 505 (p. 13 (9).

Moorman, H., and Ergermeier, J. (in Lane, J., and Epps, E., eds., 1992). "Re-structuring the schools: Problems and prospects," Berkeley: McCutchan, (pp. 15–54).

National Center for Education Statistics. (1992). "Index," Washington, D.C. The Branch.

Ordovensky, P. (in Peltier, G.) (1991). "Year-round education: The contro-versy and research evidence," *NASSP Bulletin,* v. 75, n. 536, September 1991.

Elam, S., Rose, L., and Gallup, A. (1993). "The 25th annual Phi Delta Kappa/ Gallup Poll of the public's attitude toward the public schools," *Phi Delta Kappa,* v. 75, n. 3, October 1993 (p. 143).

Toch, T. (1993). "School reform," *U.S. New and World Report,* January 11, 1991 (p. 60).

Year-Round Education: A Case for Change

by Teresa Arámbula Greenfield

Year-round education has been a fact of life in some districts for many years. The National Association for Year-Round Education estimates that over a million students in more than 200 school districts currently attend some type of year-round or extended-year school program (Natale 1992). Many or most of the programs arose in response to pressing space needs (Glines 1990; Weaver 1992); it is more economical to accommodate swelling enrollments by dividing students into several tracks that can alternately utilize existing buildings than to construct new buildings. As enrollments increase and revenues decline across the nation, it may be that increasing numbers of districts will consider adopting year-round programs of some kind.

CHARACTERISTICS OF YEAR-ROUND SCHOOLS

Year-round education (YRE) can take many forms. The two major structural variables are the school calendar and the tracking option. The calendar refers to the scheduling—but not the number—of school versus vacation days. For example, in the 45:15 plan students attend classes for nine weeks and then have a three-week vacation or "intersession" during which short classes may be offered. Tracking refers to whether all students attend school on the same schedule (single track option) or whether students are divided into several attendance groups, each of which follows a slightly different calendar so that all groups are never in school at the same time (multiple-track op-

From *The Educational Forum*, vol. 58, no. 3, spring 1994, pp. 252–62. © 1994 by Kappa Delta Pi. Reprinted with permission.

tion). Many existing plans are described in the literature, such as the 60:20 plan (12 weeks in school and 4 weeks out), the 90:30 plan (18 weeks in, 6 weeks out), the trimester system (three 16-week sessions), the quarter system (four 12-week sessions), and many more (Weinert 1987; Glines 1990; Los Angeles City Schools 1990; Herman 1991).

Because of its increasing popularity, there have been a number of studies on the academic, affective, social, and cost benefits of year-round education, but many were limited in scope and/or time and most produced mixed results. For example, some studies have suggested that YRE can enhance student achievement because students no longer experience a long summer break and/or because they attend intersession classes during the more regular school breaks; however, only some of those studies provided tangible evidence such as standardized test scores (Brekke 1984; 1985; 1990; Baker and Pelavin 1987; Ballinger 1987; 1990). Other studies have not documented any changes in student achievement (Young and Berger 1983; Utah State Board of Education 1989; Zykowski 1991; Serow 1992; White 1992). Possibly the best suggestion of the potential academic effectiveness of YRE has come from schools that serve primarily minority and socially disadvantaged students, high-risk students, or lower-achieving students in general, for whom more continuous school attendance may be particularly critical (ABT Associates 1975; Sharpes 1979; Merino 1983; Doyle and Finn 1985; Ballinger 1987; Gifford 1987).

> Because of its increasing popularity, there have been a number of studies on the benefits of year-round education.

Studies on the affective benefits of YRE have also produced mixed results, although many students, parents, and teachers believe that it improves student attitudes toward school and reduces students absenteeism (Housden and Holmes 1981; Cruz 1987; Ballinger 1987; Utah State Board of Education 1989); some studies suggest that it also has these effects on teachers (Brekke 1985). Teachers often appreciate YRE's potential for a more flexible work/vacation schedule and higher salaries (for teaching during intersession periods), and parents appreciate the option of extended, supervised child care (Doyle and Finn

1985; Baker and Pelavin 1987; Cruz 1987; White 1987). On the other hand, some teachers believe YRE to be more difficult to teach if planning and preparation have not been thorough, and more tiring if they must spend intersession breaks preparing lessons and the classroom for the upcoming school session (Young and Berger 1983; Baker and Pelavin 1987). Principals can encounter considerable administrative and fiscal problems in a YRE system, resulting in mixed administrative opinions of YRE (Young and Berger 1983). With respect to the potential social benefits of YRE, some studies have found that YRE is correlated with decreases in school vandalism, dropout rates, and disciplinary problems (Brekke 1985; Ballinger 1990; Gifford 1987; White 1987; Oxnard School District 1990).

> Some studies have found that YRE is correlated with decreases in school vandalism, dropout rates, and disciplinary problems.

One benefit that seems to be generally espoused is the potential cost-effectiveness of a multiple-track YRE system. Since once group is always on vacation, a building designed to accommodate a limited number of students can actually handle considerably more. Consequently, adopting YRE can mean avoiding or postponing having to construct, equip, and staff a new building. This can mean significant savings for a school district faced with a rapidly increasing enrollment and limited funding (Brekke 1985; White 1987), although in some cases this is only temporary (Rasberry 1992).

There are, therefore, many reasons for considering and implementing YRE programs. Although the adoption of YRE may be a straightforward decision, its actual implementation is much more complex. YRE requires a major departure from traditional practices; as such, it is an educational change effort subject to all the pitfalls experienced by other change efforts as they attempt to negotiate the stages of change. That the pitfalls are more often successful than the change efforts has been well documented: the majority of educational change efforts initiated over the years have failed to become established fixtures at their institutions (Huberman and Miles 1984). The guarantee of maximum effectiveness for YRE or any other change effort, therefore, requires the ability to thoroughly understand and apply the conditions of change, briefly summarized below.

YEAR-ROUND SCHOOLS AS EDUCATIONAL CHANGE EFFORTS

Studies on change refer to it as a process rather than an event, reflecting the complexities of its underlying activities and attitudes (Hall and Hord 1987). The key activities are often described as occurring in sequential stages: planning, adoption, implementation, and institutionalization (Fullan 1990). A problem or shortcoming at any stage can abort or alter a change effort's chances for success. For example, planning should allow those being asked to change their behaviors to work out the meaning of the change for themselves, rather than expecting them to implement an inflexible plan (Fullan and Stiegelbauer 1991). Reasons for adopting a new program can range from addressing genuine program needs to taking advantage of external funding opportunities, for which reason program adoption is not necessarily tied to program endurance (Berman and McLaughlin 1977; Huberman and Miles 1984; McLaughlin 1990).

At the implementation phase of the change effort, planning problems become evident and most efforts end, particularly when the stages and requirements of change were not fully understood or addressed. In order to enhance the probability of successful implementation, change facilitators (usually school or district administrators) must be willing and able to adequately address the time, technical, resource, and personal needs of those who are being asked to implement the change—usually teachers and perhaps parents. At a minimum, this entails the following: providing continuous pressure to implement the change while simultaneously allowing a degree of flexibility to accommodate local needs; providing sufficient fiscal, technical, temporal, and material support and resources to meet participants' needs for time, training, and practice; providing emotional support for teachers as they attempt implementation, particularly when implementation is difficult; allowing participants to have shared control of the change effort; and careful and constant coordination of the multiple activities of change as they occur (Huberman and Miles 1984; Fullan 1990; Fullan and

Miles 1992). Although these requirements are not easy to fulfill, they become even more challenging if the new program calls for changing traditions and convictions that are deeply rooted (Rossman, Corbett, and Firestone 1988).

As the result of successful implementation, a change effort can evolve into a form that is compatible with its institutional context while still remaining true to its original change intent. If at this point it finally becomes accepted as the "norm" instead of the "change," to the point of being incorporated into the district's permanent academic, personnel, and fiscal structures, it is said to have become institutionalized (Huberman and Miles 1984). As suggested earlier, very few educational change efforts make it this far; most either die out on the way or become so transformed that they begin to resemble the original practices they were designed to displace. Real change is extremely difficult to effect.

> YRE programs face some of the same potential barriers to success that are experienced by other change efforts.

YRE programs, insofar as they attempt to change major features of the school, curriculum, and instruction, face some of the same potential barriers to success that are experienced by other change efforts. Because many YRE change efforts are adopted by administrative directive based on fiscal necessity, rather than by schools and their communities based on academic or social needs, their range of barriers may be even greater. Although both types of program have been self-associated with varying degrees of program "success," the concept of success varies within the particular context of the program and its method of implementation.

A district in Hawaii decided five years ago to implement the first YRE change effort in the state; it was implemented the following year. The development of this program over its four-year exploratory period afforded an excellent opportunity to observe and compare firsthand how this YRE change effort's experiences with planning, adoption, and implementation led to the ultimate decision to institutionalize, as well as how contextual features can alter both the experiences and the decisions. In the next section the program's history of implementation and progress is discussed, and the final section integrates it with information about other YRE programs—and the change process in general—to formulate suggestions for optimizing the implementation and success of YRE programs.

HISTORY OF AN "EXPLORATORY" CASE OF YRE

The school, located in a rural, agricultural area of Maui, serves approximately 700 children in grades kindergarten through 5.

> Intersession classes were designed to combine academic remediation with enrichment activities.

The school had always enjoyed a strong positive relationship with its community. Consequently, the school's climate was friendly and supportive, and overall academic achievement was generally above district and state averages. As with many mainland schools, enrollments had been steadily increasing for several years and existing facilities had rapidly become overcrowded, factors in the consideration of multiple-track YRE as a fiscal alternative. Although YRE was selected to be the new direction of the school and the community, the decision was driven by the perception of academic and social benefits rather than by fiscal matters—a decision made possible by the availability of special funding. Accordingly, the school and community decided upon a modified single-track 45:15 YRE program including intersessions, which allowed the use of vacations and empty classrooms for optional intersession classes.

In this program, all students and teachers attended school for the same four academic quarters, and both students and teachers had the option of participating in intersession classes. Intersession classes were designed to combine academic remediation with enrichment activities not normally included in the school curriculum due to time pressures. These integrated the major content areas into hands-on lessons designed to be fun and relevant to children and were developed around an annual culturally based theme. These optional classes proved to be enormously popular with students, teachers, and parents. Nearly all students willingly enrolled repeatedly; teachers explored new thematic, integrated, active teaching strategies; and parents appreciated the extended educational time as an alternative to long summer vacations. Intersession classes also proved to require extensive time, preparation, and patience:

teachers who taught intersession classes had to learn many new strategies but had little time to plan them (hiring an intersession coordinator alleviated much of this problem); teachers who did not teach during intersessions had to become accustomed to sharing their rooms and students with intersession teachers, which could mean more work with respect to frequent room cleanup and student reorientation. Although regular school sessions were still taught in the traditional mode, many teachers also experienced an increased workload in the need to resequence lesson series to ensure their completion before the next school break.

As the major motive for restructuring and lengthening the academic calendar was the hope that it would ultimately result in a positive impact on student academic achievement, interest in school, and even school behavior, progress toward each of these goals was assessed annually for four years. As with other YRE programs, this one met some, but not all, of the expectations assigned to it. One major expectation—that student academic performance would improve—did not materialize in all the ways anticipated. That is, although both teachers and parents provided numerous accounts of observed improvement, it was not fully documented by scores on standardized tests—in this case, the Stanford Achievement Test reading, mathematics, and writing subtests. Aggregated scores on these tests were compared for the three years before YRE and the four years after YRE; data were analyzed using either analysis of variance or chi-square. Results did not demonstrate significant score increases across the years in any of the content areas. Nor did the scores of a single cohort of students, tracked for two years before and then again after YRE implementation, suggest improved academic performance across time. It is important to note, however, that only a sample of its students (third-graders) could be compared with district and state norms as well as with students from a comparison school, as wide-scale data were available only for that single grade level. Despite these limitations, there was some suggestion (statistically significant for reading) of academic "improvement," as shown in the graphs

Results did not demonstrate significant score increases across the years in any of the content areas.

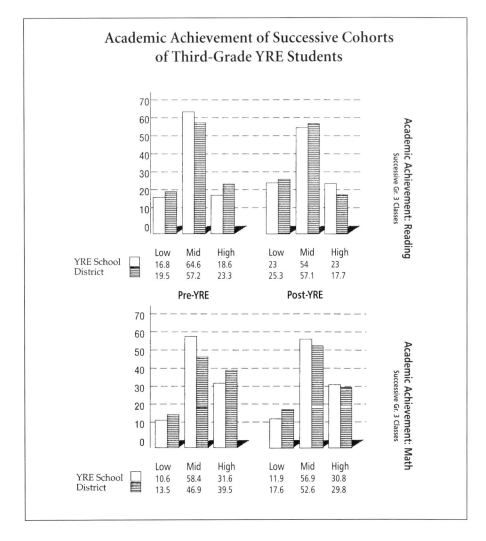

Academic Achievement of Successive Cohorts of Third-Grade YRE Students

above: although both the district and state experienced overall score decreases during these years, YRE students experienced less overall score decline, suggesting that, although scores did not actually increase, the school managed to "hold its own" by maintaining its overall scores as many others dropped theirs.

More definitive data were obtained from the summer learning-dropoff test results. The test, a locally developed and validated curriculum-based evaluation instrument, was administered to both YRE students and students at a local comparison school (selected by the district as academically and demographically comparable to the YRE school) twice each year: as a pretest during the last two weeks of the year, and as a posttest during the first two weeks of the following school year. Pretests and posttests were matched for scoring; data were analyzed using analysis of variance for a group test-sex comparisons and Sandler's A test for repeated measures comparisons. Results indicated that, although most students experienced some learning loss, YRE students experienced less and the differences were statistically significant. Although YRE students do not seem to retain what they learn better than non-YRE students do, however, any general enhancement of academic achievement was not manifested in scores on standardized tests.

> Both survey and interview results documented overwhelming student, teacher, parent, and nonteaching staff approval of YRE.

Support for a positive YRE impact on affective and social dimensions was much stronger. Information was gathered using surveys and interviews, which were locally developed and validated (using factor analysis with Varimax rotation); chi-square was used to analyze results. Follow-up interviews were done with a 20 percent sample of teachers and students; parents were not interviewed. Both survey and interview results documented overwhelming student, teacher, parent, and nonteaching staff approval of YRE over the entire time period. Students, who enjoyed YRE's more frequent vacations as well as its intersession classes, repeatedly expressed a preference for YRE over traditional-calendar school (TCS). That preference grew stronger, especially for older students, as students spent more years under YRE and memories of long summer vacations began to fade.

Teachers, twelve-month staff, and parents were asked to identify advantages and disadvantages of YRE for their own situations and their responses, aggregated over four years, are summarized in Table 1 on page 134. Although most opinions remained fairly stable over time, there were a few significant opinion shifts. For example, increasing numbers of teachers cited a greater opportunity for educational as well as vacation diversity as a YRE advantage, and fewer cited increased workload and greater intrusion on personal time as YRE disadvan-

Table 1
YRE Advantages and Disadvantages
over a Four-Year Period

Advantages for Teachers

Potential for extra salary	85.6%
More varied educational opportunities for intersessions	83.1%
More frequent, shorter vacations	82.1%
Flexible work-year length	80.0%
More varied educational opportunities for regular sessions	72.7%

Disadvantages for Teachers

Cleanup/prep during intersessions	46.7%
Less time for extended leaves	41.0%
Increased work load	40.2%**
Greater intrusion on personal time	39.7%**
Conflicting family vacation times	32.9%
More student fatigue/burnout	31.7%
More teacher fatigue/burnout	17.1%

Advantages for 12-Month Staff

More education for children	79.0%

Disadvantages for 12-Month Staff

Increased workload	33.3%**

Advantages for Parents

More education for children	93.2%
Safe, educational summer care	86.2%
More frequent, shorter vacations	74.7%
Remedial help for children	61.6%*
More varied educational opportunities	61.6%
More varied vacation opportunities	61.6%

Disadvantages for Parents

Conflicting family vacation times	20.0%**
Less chance for "summer fun"	17.9%
Less time for extended leaves	17.2%
More student fatigue/burnout	9.4%

*   Indicates significantly (alpha = .05) increased perception of advantage over time
** Indicates significantly (alpa = .05) decreased perception of disadvantage over time

tages. For parents, the major change was a decrease over time in the number citing conflicting family vacation times as a YRE disadvantage. Twelve-month staff, many of whom were initially opposed to YRE because it required extra work but did not provide extra salary, learned to accommodate their workload to fit the new schedules and thus also began to favor YRE over TCS.

Teacher and parent opinions about YRE's impact on the school and community were also positive and remained stable throughout the four-year period. Both groups believed that YRE had a positive impact on student achievement, student interest in school, and community support for the school; they also believed that YRE did not bear negative consequences for school services such as record-keeping, lunch provision, bus transportation, health services, custodial care, or school use of community resources and facilities.

The economic impact of YRE was observed by the community and state as closely as was its academic impact. Economic impact was examined with respect both to overall program cost, aggregated before and after YRE inception, and cost per pupil. Overall, YRE costs were high, which is not surprising in light of the extra school days, teacher salaries, transportation, lunches, materials, etc., involved with year-round operation. Costs were not uniformly high across the four-year period, however. Rather, YRE costs were highest initially, when the program was being set up, and subsequently demonstrated much lower annual increases. In fact, the program's annual overall cost increases—but not overall costs—declined over the years; although the average annual cost increase was around 20 percent per year over four years, actual cost increases declined from about 33 percent to 10 percent over the entire period. Per-pupil costs, while also increasing annually, showed an even more dramatic decline in rate of increase over the years, as shown in Table 2 on page 136. Despite this, the YRE program remained more expensive to operate.

On the whole, the YRE exploration was considered to be a very positive experience by both the school and community and, in fact, by many outside the community: the number of out-of-district parents sending their children to the YRE increased greatly after the program began, and schools and communities all over the state began preparations to convert to

Table 2
Changes in YRE Per-Pupil Costs over Time

Fiscal Year	Institution	Percent Annual Increase
1987–88	YRE School	NA
	District	NA
	State	NA
1988–89	YRE School	+20
	District	+9
	State	+9
1989–90	YRE School	+4
	District	+13
	State	+12
1990–91	YRE School	−1
	District	+10
	State	+8

similar YRE systems based on this exploratory project. YRE thus received strong local support during its entire pilot period: the school and community felt that YRE had indeed met their expectations. Although the anticipation of greater student academic performance was not realized in standardized test scores, this was not surprising given the nature of the standardized tests and the small sample sizes. Rather, test scores were viewed as tentative and limited, and more confidence was placed in personal observations of student success stories and parent and teacher satisfaction. However, the state was obliged to rely more heavily on the objective data and ultimately decided to drop future funding for the program. Nonetheless, the strong school and community commitment to YRE is leading them to explore other options for financial support, including grants and parent tuition for intersession classes.

IMPLICATIONS

Experiences and results of this and other YRE programs can provide guidelines to other districts contemplating YRE adoption. First, YRE programs represent major change efforts whose potential for success can be maximized by planning for them within the context of what is known about the processes and requirements of change. Second, the success of a program is a function of its context, which means that expectations for success must be carefully developed. Third, the context of the change can itself change over time, requiring a reassessment of program expectations. Each of these guidelines is discussed below.

YRE as a Change Effort

As change efforts, YRE programs must negotiate the stages of the change process, and their progress can be facilitated by an understanding of how features integral to a YRE system can serve to either enhance or diminish its potential for endurance. First, most YRE programs are administratively mandated, and, though this can ensure program adoption and implementation, it is not sufficient to ensure success, as that requires provision of essential resources for change (Huberman and Miles 1984). At a minimum, this includes provision of adequate fiscal resources to cover the increased costs associated with equipping and maintaining classrooms, paying teacher salaries, covering bus costs, etc. If instructional strategies are also targeted for change, resources must also purchase or provide the following: sufficient, relevant in-service support to allow participants to learn, practice, and receive feedback in the new practices; required instructional and technical supplies and information; and emotional support as participants struggle through the early and most difficult stages of implementation (Huberman and Miles 1984). With adequate time and resource support, participants can personalize the change such that the change itself and not a mandate ultimately becomes the major motivation.

Second, most YRE programs are designed to target only the school calendar; however, if the school hopes to improve academic achievement, it must simultaneously target curriculum and instruction, as simply applying a new calendar to old strategies will not improve instruction. Such comprehensive change efforts are more likely to lead to significant change (Fullan and Stiegelbauer 1991), but they also make the change effort more complex and difficult to implement, negatively affecting endurance because so many things are being simultaneously changed in major ways. This requires a change facilitator with the ability and power to ensure program implementation, assess and provide needed resources, coordinate the multiple dimensions and activities,

Community needs other than fiscal constraints should be assessed when YRE is being considered as a local change option.

facilitate communication between all parties, and serve as the stabilizing force for the effort. This very demanding role is often assumed by the principal in addition to regular administrative duties that are already multiplied by the increase in school sessions. Maximization of the chances for comprehensive program change and endurance, therefore, requires a principal and assistants able and willing to invest considerable time and energy in the program.

Third, YRE programs invariably exert a major impact not only on schools but also on their communities; the communities, in turn, can positively or negatively affect YRE. For example, a community's desire to provide more educational opportunities for children, add local cultural enrichment to the curriculum, or address special needs students, may lead to a district's decision to include intersession classes specially designed to address those needs (Natale 1992). On the other hand, a community may feel that YRE does not meet its needs and oppose it before it even begins (Sardo-Brown and Rooney 1992). Because of this, community needs other than fiscal constraints should be assessed when YRE is being considered as a local change option, perhaps by means of mail or telephone surveys, media campaigns, or town meetings. The increased costs associated with identifying and addressing community needs may ultimately pay off in increased community support for the school, as happened with the school and community profiled in this study.

YRE as a Function of Context

Experiences of YRE programs have confirmed that the success of a program is a function of its context, and that expectations for success must therefore be developed carefully. What works for one district may not work for another because their situations are too different. Therefore, basing program expectations on another district's successes is unrealistic. This includes expectations such as cost savings (which are realized primarily by multiple-track YRE programs experiencing tremendous growth, and not by single-track systems or those with stable or declining growth patterns), improved academic performance (which is realized primarily by YRE programs that have added remedial intersession classes and/or have changed basic instructional methods), staff support (which is generated and mobilized by a committed and capable administrative leader), and community support (which is most likely when the program was designed to meet community needs). For YRE to "succeed" within a particular context, program goals must be developed and evaluated within the limitations of that context.

Change in the YRE Context

The context of the changed can itself change over time, requiring a reassessment of program expectations. In one program (White 1992), YRE was discontinued after a 14-year implementation period due in part to changing context. Although the major contextual basis for YRE—a classroom fiscal shortage—did not actually change over the years, both the school board's priorities and the community's feelings did. While a district cannot anticipate the directions in which its community or environment will move, it can be open to the idea that change plans must sometimes be altered to address changing priorities. When that occurs, it is time to reevaluate the original reasons for adopting YRE as well as to reassess current school and community needs, and then develop a new program direction within the context of the research on effective schools and change.

In summary, YRE is a wide-scale educational change effort that is becoming increasingly popular as its major context—reduced budgets and welling school enrollments—becomes more common. As more schools turn to YRE to address their fiscal problems, they may also wish to maximize its effectiveness by addressing other educational problems as well through knowledge and application of the requirements and processes of change.

REFERENCES

ABT Associates. 1975. *Year-round schools, final report: The importance of year-round schools, vol. II.* Cambridge, Mass.: ABT Associates, Inc.

Baker, K., and S. Pelavin. 1987. *Some effects of year round school.* Washington, D.C.: Pelavin Associates.

Ballinger, C. 1987. Unleashing the school calendar. *Thrust for Educational Leadership* 16(4): 16–18.

Ballinger, C. 1990. Year-round education: Learning more for less. *Updating School Board Policies* 21(5): 1–5.

Berman, P., and M. W. McLaughlin. 1977. *Volume VII: Factors affecting implementation and continuation (Research Rep. No. R-1589/7-HEW).* Santa Monica, Calif.: RAND Corporation.

Brekke, N. R. 1984. Year round education: Cost saving and educationally effective. *Spectrum* 2(3): 25–30.

Brekke, N. R. 1985. *A cost analysis of year-round education in the Oxnard School District.* Oxnard, Calif.: Oxnard School District. ERIC, ED 272973.

Brekke, N. R. 1990. *YRE: A break from tradition that makes educational and economic sense.* Oxnard, Calif.: Oxnard School District. ERIC, ED 324818.

Cruz, J. 1987. *Implementing a year-round school—Monroe style.* Unpublished report. ERIC, ED 280187.

Doyle, D. P., and C. E. Finn, Jr. 1985. Now is the time for year-round school. *Principal* 65(1): 29–31.

Fullan, M. G. 1990. Staff development, innovation, and institutional development. In *Changing school culture through staff development,* ed. B. Joyce, 3–25. Alexandria, Va.: Association for Supervision and Curriculum Development.

Fullan, M. G., and S. Stiegelbauer. 1991. *The New meaning of educational change.* New York: Teachers College Press.

Fullan, M. G., and M. B. Miles. 1992. Getting reform right: What works and what doesn't. *Phi Delta Kappan* 73(10): 745–52.

Gifford, B. 1987. Back on the track: A campaign to recruit dropouts back into the Columbus Public Schools. Paper presented at the annual national meeting of the National School Public Relations Association, 13–16 July, at San Antonio, Tex.

Glines, D. 1990. Maximizing school capacity. *Thrust for Educational Leadership* 20(1): 49–54.

Hall, G. E, and S. M. Hord. 1987. *Change in schools: Facilitating the process.* New York: State University Press.

Herman, J. L. 1991. Novel approaches to relieve overcrowding: The effects of Concept 6 year-round schools. *Urban Education* 26(2): 195–213.

Housden, T., and L. Holmes. 1981. *Mesa Verde—a year-round high school: A descriptive report of 1980–1981.* Carmichael, Calif.: San Juan Unified School District.

Huberman, A., and M. B. Miles. 1984. *Innovation up close: How school improvement works.* New York: Plenum Press.

Los Angeles City Schools. 1990. *Models of year-round education calendars.* Los Angeles, Calif.: Los Angeles City Schools. ERIC, ED 324819.

McLaughlin, M. W. 1990. The RAND Change Agent Study revisited: Macro perspectives and micro realities. *Educational Researcher* 19(9): 11–16.

Merino, B. J. 1983. The impact of year-round schooling: A review. *Urban Education* 18(3): 298–316.

Natale, J. A. 1992. Success stories in year-round schooling. *American School Board Journal* 178(7): 29.

Oxnard School District. 1990. *Year-round education in the Oxnard School District and related YRE references.* Oxnard, Calif.: Oxnard School District. ERIC, ED 324817.

Rasberry, Q. 1992. *Year-round schools may not be the answer.* North Carolina. ERIC, ED 353558.

Rossman, G. B., H. D. Corbett, and W. A. Firestone. 1988. *Change and effectiveness in schools: A cultural perspective.* New York: State University Press.

Sardo-Brown, D., and M. Rooney. 1992. The vote on year-round schools. *American School Board Journal* 178(7): 25–27.

Serow, R. 1992. *Year-round education program: Evaluation report.* Raleigh, N.C.: Wake County Public School System.

Sharpes, D. K. 1979. Have a discipline problem? Turn to your community for help in schools. *American School Board Journal* 166(10): 30.

Utah State Board of Education. 1989. *Statewide evaluation of year-round and extended-day schools.* Salt Lake City, Utah: Utah State Board of Education. ERIC, ED 322572.

Weaver, T. 1992. *Year-round education. ERIC Digest No. 58.* Eugene, Oreg.: University of Oregon, ERIC Clearinghouse on Educational Management.

Weinert, R. 1987. Designing schools for year round education. *Thrust for Educational Leadership* 16(7): 18–19.

White, W. D. 1987. Effects of the year-round calendar on school attendance. Paper presented at the annual national meeting of the National Council on Year-Round Education, 1–4 Feb., at Anaheim, Calif.

White, W. D. 1992. Year-round no more. *American School Board Journal* 178(7): 27–30.

Young, R. J., and D. E. Berger. 1983. Evaluation of a year-round junior high school operation. *NASSP Bulletin* 67: 53-59.

Zykowski, J. L. 1991. A review of year-round education research. Riverside, Calif.: California Educational Research Cooperative. ERIC, ED 330040.

Opinions Regarding Year-Round Education: A Survey Among the Public

by Kim VanderHooven

T he purpose of this study was to compare opinions of individuals as to the benefits and drawbacks of a year-round school system. While the research that has been done on this topic provides both sides of the situation, it is obvious that proponents of year-round school feel inclined to provide more reasons for the implementation of this plan (Ballinger, 1993; Oxnard, 1992; White, 1993). It is hypothesized here that more individuals will express a desire for the implementation of year-round school, once the explanation that is included in the survey about year-round schools is read and understood. This study will investigate the opinions of individuals and determine the need for further research in this area.

> Studies of year-round schools have proven them to be cost effective if approached in the proper manner.

Studies of year-round schools have proven them to be cost effective if approached in the proper manner (Denton & Walents, 1993). The multi-track plan, as opposed to the single-track plan, can provide benefits in terms of cutting down on operating and capital costs. The potential exists for reduction of educational costs, especially in areas where population growth is a concern.

Further benefits of year around schooling include decreased drop-out rates, all-year counseling, the availability of

Unpublished paper from ERIC, 1994, ED 376 603. © 1994 by Kim VanderHooven. Reprinted with permission.

cooperative work experience, and improved staff development (White, 1993). Teachers, students, and administrators who have had the opportunity to take part in year-round school have expressed an overall satisfaction and further stated that boredom and fatigue were reduced with the shorter, more frequent vacations of the multi-track system (Barrett and others, 1992).

Both advantages and disadvantages of year-round schools are outlined in the study by Glass (1992). The advantages cited include cost-cutting, in terms of administrative costs, and less burnout among teachers and students. Disadvantages include the possible disruption of family life and the possibility that district services, such as special education and teacher workshops, may be difficult to schedule.

The study done by Rasberry (1992), defines the specific disadvantages of a year-round school. There are no guarantees that additional time will be spent on a better education and furthermore, tax support for the program may be non-existent.

The present study is a step toward increasing understanding among those who are uncertain as to the public opinion on year-round school. Although studies that researched the benefits and drawbacks of year-round school were plentiful, a public opinion survey was not as readily available. Thus, the specific purpose of this study was to obtain opinions within the framework of the general public concerning the implementation of year-round school.

METHOD
Subjects
Thirty individuals living in Northwest Ohio and Southeast Michigan were included in the sample. The individuals ranged in age from 24 to 58 and consisted of both men and women. They were chosen to participate if they expressed an interest in the topic of year-round school. This random sampling approach was utilized due to its convenient nature.

Measures
A survey was utilized to determine the general opinion of the individual participating in the study (see Appendix on page 149). A brief explanation concerning what a year-round school consists of was included in the survey, as well as a space for

comments. The participant could circle "For," "Against," or "Undecided" when asked to respond to opinion regarding year-round school.

Instruments
The survey utilized for the purpose of this study was formulated by the author. Questions were kept simple and easy to understand, since a general opinion was required. Individuals who participated in the study were given an example of a year-round school calendar and were then asked to complete the survey.

Reliability and Validity
The survey is considered to be reasonably reliable since the items included in the survey were minimal and easily understood. Errors and inconsistency could occur if the subjects were not totally honest about their opinion and were answering to go along with the status quo.
    Validity information was not available for this survey.

Procedures
The survey was given to subjects who were first asked if they would participate in a survey for educational research. The survey and purpose of the survey were then explained to the individual with an emphasis being placed on honesty in answering the questions.
    Subjects were chosen randomly over the period of one week and an emphasis was placed on choosing subjects of varying backgrounds.

RESULTS
The degree and propensity with which subjects responded to the survey was astounding. While some individuals were undecided or simply uninformed about year-round schools, most had a definite opinion and were quite willing to provide comments. Sixty percent of the subjects were "Against" the implementation of year-round schools, 27 percent were "For" year-round schools, and 13 percent were "Undecided." One individual made a valid point when she stated that "if the schools were all air-conditioned" she would be for it. Others [who] were for year-round schools believed that year-round school

would benefit the students in terms of an uninterrupted learning process. The time away from school would be less, thus increasing knowledge retention.

The individuals who were against year-round school expressed a concern with the traditional "summer vacation." One individual commented that summers are for vacation—not school. Numerous individuals also made comments to the effect that quality education was not likely to improve simply because of a change in the days that students are required to attend.

> The results of this study clearly indicate resistance to the implementation of year-round school . . . .

Individuals who remained undecided seemed to understand the benefits and drawbacks of year-round school and, having never experienced a similar situation, were unsure of the long-term effects year-round school would have on students.

The above results fail to support the hypotheses that the majority of the subjects would respond favorably to the idea of year-round school. While there are many variables to consider when changing to a year-round school, the survey failed to relate the importance of considering the benefits as well as the drawbacks when answering the questions.

DISCUSSION

The results of this study clearly indicate resistance to the implementation of year-round school in the Midwestern portion of the United States. While there may be some validity to the reasoning behind the resistance, it is believed that misinformation and resistance to change are the major influencing factors. Over 2,000 schools now use year-round education quite successfully, proving that the system can work (Ballinger, 1993). Ballinger suggests introducing the concept to the public by stressing the educational values inherent in the year-round school concept and avoiding large community meetings in the beginning stages.

The fact that 60 percent of the individuals who were surveyed were against year-round schools indicates a powerful stance among the public. The results that were obtained in a study by Barrett and others (1992), indicate a public that is quite satisfied with the year-round education system. The individuals who are currently participating in year-round education accepted the system as an alternative to overcrowding in schools and a lack of teachers. Parents and staff believed that year-round school allowed students to stay on task and retain more information. Furthermore, 90 percent of the staff were satisfied overall with year-round education. Perhaps if the same situation were to occur in the Midwest, and year-round education was the only alternative, the public would be more willing to accept year-round school.

In support of the individuals who were against year-round education, Rasberry (1992), researched drawbacks of the system. Results of this study included an increase in dropout rates, diminished student employment opportunities, and less growth and development time for children. Furthermore, it was stated that extra time may not necessarily be used for better education. This statement supports the concerns of individuals that were included in this study.

Implications
The results of this study indicate that the public has definite views in terms of year-round education. Very few individuals were undecided (13%), while the remaining individuals were adamant about their opinions. Individuals undertaking research in this area should be aware of the fact that this subject may elicit strong opinions—whether they are for or against the implementation of year-round education.

Summary
It should be taken into consideration that year-round education is still a relatively new concept in the Midwestern portion of the United States. Many individuals are unaware of the benefits year-round education can provide. Advantages such as decreased drop-out rates and less burnout among teachers and students are important factors to consider. Furthermore, there is a distinct possibility that students will retain more knowledge, since the break between classes is less than three months. All of these factors point to how advantageous year-round education can be. However, without the support of parents and the com-

munity, year-round school may not get a chance to be implemented in this area.

REFERENCES

Ballinger, C. (1993). *Annual report to the Association on the status of Year-Round Education.* Paper presented at the annual meeting of the National Association for Year-Round Education. Las Vegas, NV. (ERIC Document Reproduction Service No. ED 358 551)

Barrett, T., and others. (1992). *Results of the Year-Round Education Parent, Staff, and Student Surveys.* Riverside Unified School District, CA. (ERIC Document Reproduction Service No. ED 358 562)

Denton, J. J., & Walents, B. (1993). *Cost analysis of year round schools: Variables and algorithms.* (ERIC Document Reproduction Service No. ED 358 515)

Glass, G. V. (1992). *Policy considerations in conversion to Year-Round schools.* Arizona State University, AZ. (ERIC Document Reproduction Service No. ED 357 476)

Oxnard School District. (1992). *What YRE can do to enhance academic achievement and to enrich the lives of students that the traditional calendar cannot do.* Oxnard School District, CA. (ERIC Document Reproduction Service No. ED 352 223)

Rasberry, Q. (1992). *The extended school year: Is more necessarily better?* (ERIC Document Reproduction Service No. ED 353 657)

White, W. D. (1993). *Educational benefits in Year-Round High Schools.* Paper presented at the annual meeting of the National Association for Year-Round Education. Las Vegas, NV. (ERIC Document Reproduction Service No. ED 359 660)

Appendix

Survey of Opinions Regarding Year-Round Education

The following is a survey that is being conducted for educational research. Your answers are confidential. Please be as truthful as possible when answering. Thank you for your help.

What is your gender?   male   female

What is your age? _____

Introduction

In year-round schools, as in traditional nine-month schools, students attend classes about 180 days of the year. In the most popular year-round plan, four groups of students attend school for nine weeks, and then have fifteen days off.

What is your opinion regarding year-round school? (Please circle the appropriate response.)

FOR   AGAINST   UNDECIDED

Comments:

Year-Round Schooling as an Avenue to Major Structural Reform

by Patricia Gándara and Judy Fish

This article reports on a study that sought to experiment with multiple education reforms in the context of an extended school calendar year. Three schools, with very different characteristics, undertook to extend their school year to approximately 223 days (from the previous 180 days), reorganize funding to provide more days of schooling for many students, and increase the length of the work year, and consequently the salaries of teachers. All three schools were able to demonstrate increases in academic achievement, a high level of parent and teacher satisfaction, and a cost-effective use of existing school facilities. Implications for education reform and year-round schooling are discussed.

After more than a decade of declining test scores and increasing criticism of public education, the 1980s saw the beginning of a virtual storm of proposals for reforming, restructuring, and reinventing American education. By 1989, state and federal government agencies had issued more than 300 reports suggesting what ought to be done to improve school performance (Alliance for Achievement, 1989), and the flood of reports and plans has continued unabated (Cuban, 1992). Many of the suggestions have focused on strengthening accountability of both students and teachers, increasing graduation and proficiency requirements, enriching the curriculum, and restructuring power relationships among schools, parents, and teachers (Alliance for Achievement, 1989; Cuban, 1992; Stedman & Jor-

From *Educational Evaluation and Policy Analysis,* vol. 16, no. 1, spring 1994, pp. 67–85. © 1994 by the American Educational Research Association. Reprinted with permission.

dan, 1986). All of these ideas appear to hold promise, and a large body of literature suggests that, when implemented well, each could contribute to a better functioning educational system. One maxim in education, however, is that innovation or reform works best (and sometimes works *only*) when it is adapted to the specific context in which it is to be implemented (McLaughlin, 1987).

California, like the rest of the nation, is facing serious challenges to its educational system. Schools are overcrowded and growing at an unprecedented pace—approximately 200,000 additional students annually (Gordon, 1991); class sizes are among the highest in the nation (Policy Analysis for California Education [PACE], 1991); one out of five students does not speak English (California Department of Education, 1991); a significant portion (estimated at about 30%) of students continue to show a decline in test scores relative to the total school population (Brown & Haycock, 1984; PACE, 1991); and the state has anticipated growing shortages of qualified teachers, especially those trained to deal with special populations (Cagampang, Garms, Greenspan, & Guthrie, 1985; PACE, 1991). Moreover, many school districts have been wracked in recent years by teacher strikes for higher pay and better working conditions. This litany of problems could be divided into three categories: *pedagogical,* that is, what and how students at risk for school failure are taught; *teacher compensation and working conditions;* and *facilities,* or where and how students are housed.

The major response by the state to these pedagogical issues has been the creation of various "categorical programs" to provide more resources for students with exceptional educational needs, such as language and learning differences and socioeconomic disadvantage. The typical categorical program pulls students out of the regular classroom for some portion of the day or week to receive special services (Gartner & Lipsky, 1987). In theory, this not only provides additional educational benefit to the child, but reduces the burden on the teacher as well. In reality, however, the child misses out on whatever is going on in the regular classroom while being served in the "pull-out," and teachers complain that they lose continuity of instruction. Furthermore, this strategy requires the child to be segregated from peers during portions of the day and results in children being labeled as different. Not surprisingly, research has shown that such programming not only is often ineffective but is occasionally harmful to educationally disadvantaged students (Gartner & Lipsky, 1987; Kimbrough & Hill, 1981).

Teacher compensation and working conditions are largely local issues, with only limited regulation by the state; hence, state policy has had little direct impact on them. Nonetheless, teacher salaries have been increasing, albeit incrementally. Average teacher salaries in California rose from $18,020 in 1979–1980 to $38,996 in 1989–1990. This represented a 32% constant-dollar increase during the decade (Snyder & Hoffman, 1991). Salaries have continued to grow at a rate higher than inflation, reaching a mean salary of $41,811 for the 1991–1992 school year (California Department of Education, 1992). The issue of class size, however, continues to be a grave concern of teachers (McDonnell & Pascal, 1988). Unfortunately, it is virtually impossible to achieve a reduction in class size within the current system because of enormous costs and inadequate facilities. Even if the money were available to pay the salaries of all of the additional teachers required to reduce class size, there would be no place to house the students removed from existing classrooms.

> It is virtually impossible to achieve a reduction in class size within the current system.

With respect to facilities issues, the major state response to overcrowding has been (a) a series of always-inadequate bond proposals to build more schools and (b) new laws that provide both incentives for converting to multitrack year-round operation and penalties for not doing so. The result has been a steady increase in the numbers of schools converting to year-round operation. In 1988, 7.7% of the state's public school students attended year-round schools; 4 years later, in 1992, 25% of students were in year-round schools (Payne, personal communication, quoted from the current database of the California State Department of Education, April 1, 1992).

Given the intransigence of many of the pedagogical and teacher working conditions issues, and the inevitability of increased year-round operation of schools, it is important to understand how these factors might co-vary. The study reported in this article was designed to explore those relationships. Specifically, it tested the possibility of providing teaching and learning conditions for both students and teachers—in the context of a particular kind of year-round program—that would be substantially better than those offered in either traditional schools or in year-round schools whose sole purpose was to accommodate more students.

The working hypothesis was that it is possible to reorganize school calendars and existing resources in a way that will give schools greater flexibility in programming, provide teachers a more rewarding compensation, and enhance the education of the most "at risk" learners without compromising the education of the total student body, and it would accomplish this in a fashion that actually served some of the compelling needs of the state (e.g., housing additional students and creating incentives for teachers to remain in the workforce). This experiment came to be known as the Orchard Plan.

THE STUDY

Four elementary schools (including one K–8) in different parts of the state were selected through a competitive proposal review process, by the Department of Education, to participate in this study. Three schools fully implemented the program and remained with the study for its duration.

The schools were selected in the spring of 1988 and were given a grant of $60,000 each to spend during the 1988–1989 school year to include school and district staff, parents, and community in developing a plan to convert to an extended year operation[1] that would include certain key features specified in a contract with the district. Schools began implementation during the 1989–1990 school year. In that year, and in 1990–1991, schools were each granted an additional $60,000 to move to the new program and to cover some costs associated with the study. While expenditures were left entirely to the discretion of the schools, most chose to spend their money on setting up a data collections system, computerizing their curricula, and providing release time for their teachers to plan.

Schools were asked to adopt a 60-15 year-round schedule in which five heterogeneously assembled groups (or "tracks") would attend school for 60 days, then have vacation, or attend intersession, for 15 days. This cycle was to be repeated three times during the school year. All students and teachers, however, would share a common summer break of approximately 4 weeks, plus 2 weeks at winter and a 1-week spring vacation. Research suggests that the resulting shortened vacations should have a positive effect on student achievement, particularly for educationally "disadvantaged" students. It has been hypothesized that this would occur because there would be less learning loss over the shorter breaks as well as because teachers would need to spend less time reviewing previously taught material (Handleman & Harris, 1984; New York State Department of Education & State University of New York, 1978; Quinlan, 1987).

> Shortened vacations should have a positive effect on student achievement.

Although five tracks (of approximately seven students each) are assigned to a single teacher and all of the students will eventually have contact with each other, only four tracks are present at any one time. Figure 1 on page 157 presents a graphic illustration of this scheduling pattern.

This configuration results in a reduction in class size of about 3 students. For example, a teacher who may have once had 31 students in his or her class would now have 35 on the roster, but only 28 would be in class at any one time ($35 \div 5 = 7$; $7 \times 4 = 28$). It also results in a constantly changing classroom dynamic, a feature that will be discussed later.

Another critical element of the study was the reorganization of existing categorical funds. Schools were invited to use any categorical funding they chose (which could include such things as economic impact aid, special education, summer school funds, etc.) to support innovative intersession programs to be offered especially, but not exclusively, to targeted students (those deemed most at risk for school failure) during intersession (3-week break) periods. The intent was to reduce or eliminate pull-out instruction in favor of intensive blocks of enriched educational experiences every 3 months. Schools were to be monitored to ensure that the most at-risk students were served and that the intersession programming would be sufficient in both quality and quantity; however, the content and structure of such programming, as well as its source of funding, were left to the discretion of the individual schools.

Schools were to be monitored to ensure that the most at-risk students were served.

Another element of the experiment was to involve teachers: the way they structure teaching and the way they are compensated for their work. A number of studies have concluded that cooperative teaching and learning strategies can have a positive effect on student achievement (Cohen, 1972; Lyman & Foyle, 1990; Oakes, 1985; Slavin, 1990). The Orchard Plan consists of structural incentives for teachers to team-teach and to organize their students into cooperative learning groups. With different tracks of students moving in and out of the classroom every 3 weeks, whole group instruction loses its attractiveness. Instead, to accommodate the rotating tracks, teachers naturally gravitate to 3-, 6-, or 9-week instructional blocks designed for smaller subgroups of students. If these are well implemented, the result should be a carefully planned curriculum, a well-paced instructional delivery, and better monitoring of individual student progress.

Studies of teacher attrition rates (Cagampang, Garms, Greenspan, & Guthrie, 1985; Darling-Hammond, 1984) suggest that as many as half the teachers in the teaching force leave teaching within any 7-year period. Desire for a higher salary is one of the primary reasons given (Murnane, Singer, Willet, Kemple, & Olsen, 1991). Hence, another feature of the experiment was to allow teachers to be paid 20% more than they would have earned in a traditional school, by lengthening their contracts.[2] In virtually all cases, this could represent a very competitive salary in the job market. Additionally, since 20% more pupils could be taught with the same number of teachers, schools would realize a savings in benefit costs, (usually about

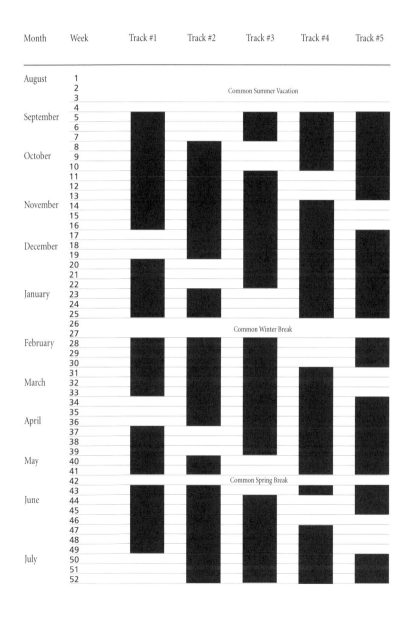

Figure 1
Proposed Year-Round School Schedule

Table 1
Elements of the Orchard Plan Experiment

1. An extended year calendar in which approximately 223 days are available for instruction.

2. A reorganization of categorical funding (e.g., Chapter 1, economic impact aid, special education, gifted and talented) to shift these funds into intersession enrichment courses, thereby providing extra days of instruction, with emphasis on at-risk students.

3. A reduction in class size by at least two to three students per classroom, achieved through a rotation of five tracks of students in which only four tracks are present at any one time. (Teachers have 20% more students on their rolls, but about three students fewer in their class at any time.)

4. The accommodation of 20% more students at the site.

5. The opportunity for teachers to extend the length of their contracts by 20%, resulting in 20% higher salaries.

6. The restructuring of the curriculum into smaller units with built-in review and more careful monitoring of student progress. (Team teaching, small group learning experiences, and mastery-learning orientation are expected to result from this restructuring.)

7. Voluntary participation on the part of schools, teachers, and families with all having a stake in the planning of the program.

30% of salary) for every new teacher not hired. These savings could then be redirected back into the schools' programs.

Having teachers on extended year contracts while students rotate in and out of school meant that, unlike other multitrack year-round plans, teachers would never change classrooms—a common complaint of year-round schooling (see Table 1).

These were the principal features of the study; as each school adapted its plan to meet its own needs, each developed features characteristic of its own circumstances. These are discussed later in the section on findings.

THE STUDY SAMPLE[3]
Lark School
Lark is a small rural school serving approximately 245 children in Grades K–6 (one classroom per grade level). It is located in

an economically depressed area in the rural north of the state, and 90% of the students are on Aid for Dependent Families (AFDC) or the school's free lunch program. Approximately half of the students are ethnic minorities, with 20% of the population being Hmong. At least 10% of the students are Limited English Proficient (LEP). The school has had a high transiency rate, losing about one third of its students each year. However, it had also been experiencing overcrowding, which required neighborhood children to be bused away from the school, hence the interest in converting to a multitrack year-round operation that would increase the school's capacity.

The small staff, with the exception of one teacher, all began teaching at Lark in 1988 when the study began. (The other six members of the original staff decided they did not want to be involved in the study.) Perhaps in part because of this, there is a strong sense of cohesion among teaching staff. It is also noteworthy that the small school has suffered more than its share of turmoil. During the last 2 years, the school lost its principal to a sudden life-threatening illness, and one of the classrooms teachers stepped in as interim principal. This required adding a new teacher in midyear. During the same period two teachers became pregnant, with the result of higher than normal teacher absences. However, no teacher chose to leave the school during the period of the experiment.[4]

Palm Avenue School
Palm Avenue School is a large "magnet" school (1,100 students in K–8) located in a lower middle-class suburb of Los Angeles. It is in a rapidly growing community where overcrowding of facilities has become an acute problem. The majority of students in the school are Anglo-American, and only about 14% are minorities, mostly Hispanic. The student population is relatively stable with 90% of the students remaining from one year to the next. While the majority of students are not at risk as at Lark, about 14% of the students have been identified as Chapter 1 eligible (performing below the 35th percentile on standardized tests of academic achievement).

The staff at Palm Avenue is large, enthusiastic, and stable. Few teachers chose to leave when the study began and only one teacher was lost during the first 2 years of implementation, due to a spouse's job transfer. Teachers appear to work well together and have formed effective grade level teams.

Brady School

Brady School is located in the far southern portion of the state in a working-class urban/suburban neighborhood. It has approximately 600 students, 65% of whom are ethnic minorities, the largest group being Hispanic. Between one fourth and one fifth of the school population is LEP. Nearly 50% are on the free or reduced-fee lunch program. The official stability rate of students is about 75% (June to September); however, there is considerable movement of children in and out of school during the year, a phenomenon that is at least partially related to its proximity to the Mexican border.

Brady School had already experimented quite successfully with a single-track year-round calendar,[5] but, like the other schools, was overcrowded and turning students away. Teachers in this school were opposed to a year-round system that would have required them to continually change classrooms and so saw the Orchard experiment as having a significant advantage over other year-round schedules, which required the rotation of teachers through classrooms. Additionally, many of the teachers had taught for a number of years and had reached a place on the district pay scale where the 20% increase represented a substantially higher salary. Teachers at Brady freely admit that the salary has been a potent element in their high level of satisfaction with their jobs. Only one teacher has left the school since the experiment began.

METHODS
Monitoring Implementation

Clearly, the first critical piece of information necessary to make a judgment about the feasibility of combining the various elements discussed into real school reform was how, and how well, the plan had been implemented at each of the sites. It was, in fact, through the monitoring of implementation that the decision was made to drop one of the original four sites from the study. It became clear by the second year that this site had not wholly committed to full implementation of the program. Due to many competing programs at the school, including a teacher education center that trained 25 student teachers each year and used most of the classroom space, the intersession program was never developed and the reorganization of categorical funding never took place.

In order to monitor implementation, the first author and the program monitor for the Department of Education met regularly with school staff and administrators beginning during the planning year (1988–1989) to observe and discuss the development of plans and their implementation. We also made regular site visits to the schools, observing classrooms, other facilities, and intersession programs, and holding teacher-only and parent-only meetings to gauge the feelings of these constituent groups about the progress and effectiveness of the experiment and to ask for suggestions on how to improve it. These open and frank meetings also gave both staff and parents a greater feeling of ownership of the project.

> Open and frank meetings gave both staff and parents a greater feeling of ownership of the project.

In addition to meetings and site visits, specific implementation (and outcome) criteria had been established in the legislation that funded the experiment. These criteria assumed that the school had made the initial adjustments to the new calendar and organization of students, and consisted of the following:

1. Pupil capacity of the school should be increased by at least 18% above the baseline year.

2. Annual teacher salaries should be increased by at least 20% over the normal salary the teacher would have been paid under the traditional contract.

3. Class size would be reduced by a minimum of three pupils.

4. At least 50 hours of instructional activities during intersession should be provided for every student otherwise eligible for categorical funding. That is, the equivalent of approximately 8 additional days of instruction should be provided for all at-risk students.

5. The school, after initial start-up costs, should be able to operate this program at no additional cost, and should realize

Table 2
Demographics of Experimental and Control Schools
1988–1989

School	Students Total no.	% minority	SES percentile rank	% LEP at third grade
Lark	207	34	13	20
Control for Lark	473	29	27	0
Brady	491	65	29	13
Control for Brady	523	69	62	15
Palm	590	12	69	1.3
Control for Palm	501	30	65	1.4

some savings from the reduction in teacher benefit costs (due to the fact that fewer teachers would be serving more students).

Data relevant to these questions were collected on an annual basis at each of the schools.

Assessing Program Effectiveness

For the purposes of assessing program effectiveness, each experimental school was paired with a control school in the same district. The control schools were selected on the basis of having demographic profiles similar to the experimental schools (see Table 2). In each case, ethnic and socioeconomic status of student populations and standardized test scores were matched.

As with the assessment of program implementation, criteria were established at the outset of the study to judge the effectiveness of the program. These criteria consisted of the following:

1. Achievement of all pupils in the experiment school (measured by standardized tests) should equal or exceed that of the pupils in the control school.

2. At-risk pupils targeted for intersession instruction should show significantly greater academic growth than a comparable group of students in the control school.

3. Pupil and teacher absentee rates should not exceed the level established at the baseline year.

4. At least 60% of parents and teachers should express satisfaction with the program.

At each school, both reading and math standardized test scores were collected for a random sample of all students (minus targeted students) and for targeted at-risk students at all grade levels except kindergarten, beginning in the baseline year, 1988–1989. During the first 2 years of data collection, this included the Comprehensive Test of Basic Skills (CTBS) at Lark, the Stanford Achievement Test (SAT) at Brady, and the 3R's Test at Palm Avenue. In the 3rd year, Palm Avenue and its control changed to the CTBS, which made it impossible to compare scores over the 4-year period at this site.

With respect to notions of *at risk*, each school defined this population somewhat differently, but in a manner consistent with its own circumstances. At Lark, the total school population was considered to be at risk; hence, both of the first two effectiveness criteria (whole-school and at-risk achievement performance) could be assessed using the same sample of students. However, a separate analysis was conducted of students who had attended intersession classes for at least 10 hours during each year. Scores of both the total school population and the intersession students were compared against the same comparison group at the control school.

At Brady, separate analyses were conducted of test scores for Chapter 1 and LEP students who attended intersessions, and comparisons were made with Chapter 1 and LEP students at the control school.

At Palm Avenue, Chapter 1 students who had been targeted for intersession were analyzed separately from the total school population and compared with Chapter 1 students in the control school.

In addition to the meetings held with parents and teachers, and a survey instrument administered annually by the researcher for the first 3 years of operation, schools were charged

Table 3
Growth in School Capacity
1988–1989 to 1990–1991

School	1988–1989	1989–1990	1990–1991	% increase 1988–1989 to 1990–1991
Lark	207	230	245	18
Brady	491	596	600	22
Palm	590	906	1,100	86[a]

[a] Palm Avenue School moved to two different campuses during this period to accommodate more of the hundreds of students on waiting lists to get into the school.

with surveying the attitudes of their parents. Schools took this charge very seriously and collected copious data on parent attitudes, concerns, and desires for improvement. One school even surveyed the parents in the community who *did not* send their children to the school to find out why they had made this decision. Moreover, while not requested to do so, all schools surveyed the attitudes of their students about the program.

FINDINGS
Implementation Variables
School Capacity and Teacher Salaries
As noted earlier, one of the four schools selected for the study failed to meet critical implementation criteria and was therefore eliminated. Of the remaining three schools, all successfully reorganized their programs, increased their student populations by at least 18% (see Table 3), and increased their teacher salaries by 20% over the pay for an equivalent "traditional" teaching position in their district. Pay scales differ dramatically by district and according to years of experience within a district. Hence, the variation in the salaries of study teachers is great; however, the highest paid teachers in 1992 were making almost $70,000 per year.

**Table 4
Average Class Size
1988–1989 to 1990–1991**

School	1988–1989	1989–1990	1989 to 1990 difference	1990–1991	1989 to 1991 difference
Lark	29.6	26.2	–3.4	26.6	–3.0
Brady	30.6	26.4	–4.2	27.5	–3.1
Palm	28.7	27.3	–1.4	28.0	–0.7

Class Size

Class sizes were also reduced by at least three students in two of the schools and were reduced slightly at the third school (Palm Avenue), which had previously negotiated a class size cap of 28.5 students with its administration (see Table 4).

Intersession Programming

Schools have had varying success with their intersession programs. Clearly, this proved to be the biggest challenge for implementation. However, all three schools did *offer* at least 50 hours of additional instruction to at-risk students. The difficulty in many cases was in getting the students who could most benefit from the instruction to return to school during the intersession break. Sometimes this reflected a lack of interest, but it was also due to child-care coordination and transportation problems that low income parents encountered.

At Lark School, approximately 25% of the students in Grades 1 to 5 attend intersession programming sometime during the year. Much of the program focus has been on the Hmong and LEP students. The intersession programs have consisted of projects and activities such as kite making, skills review, and field trips. The programs have not been developed to the level that the staff would like because of space limitations, resource limitations, and unavailability of persons to coordinate the program. With such a small staff (seven teachers), this school has been particularly disadvantaged with respect to "personpower." In part the intersession program has consisted of allowing children to return to school for "informal" instruction such as "auditing" in their regular classrooms. A number of the children have, in fact, been at school for more than 220 days during the year. Interestingly, even with the limitations on the program, Lark is the only school to demonstrate statistically significant gains in achievement for its intersession students.

> Enrichment activities typically consist of readers' theatre workshops, self-esteem workshops, or mural painting.

At Brady School, 44% of the students in Grades 1 to 6 enrolled in intersession programming (and had an 80% attendance rate) during the first year. Programming consisted of math and reading reinforcement, art, literature, physical education, and computer activities. In subsequent years, the school shifted much of its intersession focus to programs serving the rapidly growing LEP population of the school. This programming has emphasized high-intensity English vocabulary building for its LEP students and has placed more emphasis on a cross-age tutoring program, bringing students on intersession back into the classrooms to work with other students. The principal and staff have reported a great deal of satisfaction with the program.

In sheer numbers, Palm Avenue has probably been the most successful in its intersession programming. Approximately 70% of the students have returned to school for some intersession instruction. The program is offered to all students, with a special focus on attracting students with special needs. Pupils have the option of returning to school, or other locations, for scheduled, full-day enrichment and extension activities, remediation, and field trips, and to serve as tutors across campus. Enrichment activities typically consist of readers' theatre workshops, self-esteem workshops, or mural painting.

With respect to special needs students, 30% of the Chapter 1 students at Palm have returned to school for extra help, and 50% of these students have returned to join one of the enrichment or extension classes during intersession. The principal has also reported an increasing number of requests from classroom teachers to keep particular students during the intersession break for "reteaching." Because the percentage of Chapter 1 pupils returning for intersession programming is less than for the school as a whole, teachers have expressed a concern about curtailing regular session pull-outs for these targeted students.

Program Costs

Data were not systematically collected on operational costs for the sites, in large part because fiscal responsibilities were divided differently among the school districts, making it difficult to track all revenue sources and expenditures at the level of detail we would have needed to make sense of the data. However, the reader will recall that the criterion for cost-effectiveness set out at the beginning of the study was that the schools would be able to operate successfully (carry out the same program) without any additional financial help from the state after the initial 3-year transition period. All schools have met this criterion. Moreover, all contend that savings derived from the reduction in teacher hires have been returned to the school to support the intersession programming. While we have no hard data to prove these assertions, given the crisis in school funding that has occurred in California, there would be no reason for a district to continue supporting a school program that was not cost-effective or that placed an additional burden on district funds.

Summary of Implementation Variables

Overall, the three project schools have been extremely successful in implementing the program. Virtually all of the implementation criteria have been met. Variations in implementation occur mostly in the areas of instructional delivery and intersession programming. Teachers at Palm Avenue do extensive team teaching within grade levels, and all schools have adopted small groups as a strategy for teaching students who are at different places in the curriculum. Schools vary in their use of 3-, 6-, or 9-week curricular units. Intersession programming has more and more reflected the special needs of the populations being served at each site.

Program Outcomes

Achievement Data

There were three questions to be answered by the achievement data: (a) Were the experimental and control schools comparable at the beginning of the study? (b) Did the Orchard experiment have any effect on the overall student achievement at the experimental schools? (c) Did the Orchard experiment have any effect on the student achievement of those students especially targeted by the program (*at risk* as defined by each school)?

Initial differences. In order to establish the comparability of the experimental and control schools, 1988–1989 baseline reading and math achievement scores of a random sample of students across grades were compared using two-sample *t* tests for each of the three sets of experimental and control schools. No differences were found between any of the sets of schools on either reading or math scores. This corroborated our earlier matching of schools based on highly similar demographic features.

Overall achievement. To answer the second question relating to overall achievement, reading and math scores were compared for matched samples of nontargeted students at each of the experimental and control pairs, using a generalized block-design analysis of variance where school was the main effect and students' grade placement at the beginning of the study was the block. The decision to block on grade level was made to control for potential teacher and cohort effects.

Four years of test scores were collected at each site; however, due to high student attrition, the *N* for matched samples became too small in the 4th year to yield a reliable analysis. Moreover, Palm Avenue School had changed its districtwide achievement test in the 1990–1991 school year, making comparisons with previous years impossible. Hence, the 2-year pretest/posttest gain scores in both math and reading for the years 1988–1989 to 1990–1991 were compared for Lark and Brady and their controls, and 1-year gain scores, 1990–1991 to 1991–1992, were compared for Palm Avenue and its control school (see Table 5).

As Table 5 shows, no significant differences were noted for either reading or math gain scores for the matched samples of students at Brady or Palm Avenue, although there was a sub-

Table 5
Mean NCE Gain Scores for Whole School in Reading and Math for Matched Samples in Experimental and Control Schools

School, test, population, and time period	Experimental		Control			
	N	$\bar{X}$ Gain	N	$\bar{X}$ Gain	F	$\bar{X}$
Lark, CTBS, intersession, 1989–1991						
Reading	24	1.98	86	−1.43	1.01	.31
Math	23	1.08	90	−8.25	4.04	.04*
Brady, SAT, LEP, 1989–1991						
Reading	33	3.23	44	4.13	0	.944
Math	33	9.78	44	8.52	0	.958
Palm, CTBS, Chapter 1, 1991–1992						
Reading	42	8.02	50	1.20	3.41	.06
Math	43	9.34	50	2.02	2.62	.10

*$p = <.05$.

stantial difference in scores, bordering on significant, for reading ($p = .06$) in favor of Palm Avenue. There was a significant difference, however, in the gains made by Lark students on math posttest scores ($p = .04$).

In sum, to answer the question "Were overall achievement scores affected by the Orchard experiment?," an analysis of variance of gains in math and reading scores suggests that there were no significant differences between the experimental and control schools, with the exception of Lark, which posted significant gains in math achievement for its student body as a whole when compared with its control school.

Achievement of targeted students. Each experimental school defined its targeted population differently. At Lark, with extremely high rates of poverty and underachievement, the whole school population was considered to be at risk and was offered intersession and/or other extended year opportunities on a first-come, first-served basis. At Brady, the staff focused on low

Table 6
Mean NCE Gain Scores for Target Students in Reading and Math for Matched Samples in Experimental and Control Schools

School, test, population, and time period	Experimental		Control			
	N	$\bar{X}$ Gain	N	$\bar{X}$ Gain	F	$\bar{X}$
Lark, CTBS, intersession, 1989–1991						
Reading	29	7.89	86	−1.43	−8.85	.003*
Math	28	11.58	90	−8.25	39.52	.0001**
Brady, SAT, LEP, 1989–1991						
Reading	26	9.26	30	1.10	4.70	.03*
Math	25	7.76	30	6.46	0.15	.69
Palm, CTBS, Chapter 1, 1991–1992						
Reading	30	11.23	36	.916	7.73	.007*
Math	30	5.46	36	4.66	.50	.48

$*p = <.05.$

achieving LEP students through its intersession program. Palm Avenue saw its Chapter 1 students (students performing below the 35th percentile in one or more academic areas) as its most at-risk population and provided both enrichment and remediation through intersession programming for them. The third question we asked of these achievement data, then, was, "To what extent did the Orchard experiment affect the achievement of the most at risk students in the school?"

To answer the question of achievement gains for targeted students, we conducted a generalized block-design analysis of variance, again blocking on grade level. As noted in Table 6, at each experimental school, the students for whom special programming had been targeted did, indeed, demonstrate significant achievement gains.

At Lark, the intersession students posted significant gains in both reading ($p = .003$) and math ($p = .0001$) on the CTBS for the period 1988–1989 to 1990–1991. At Brady, the most highly targeted group, the LEP students, showed significant gains in reading achievement on the SAT ($p = .03$) when compared with LEP students at the control school. (Not shown in the table, but of interest, was the fact that non-LEP Chapter 1 students, for whom intersession programming was also provided, did not show significant gains in either math or reading scores.) At Palm Avenue, although data were only interpretable for a 1-year period, the Chapter 1 students demonstrated a significant gain ($p = .007$) in CTBS reading scores when compared with the Chapter 1 control students.

Achievement score summary. Lark was the only school to post significant gains for the total school when compared with its control school, and this was only in math achievement. All other comparisons were nonsignificant. However, each of the experimental schools did, indeed, show significant differences in achievement gains for its most highly targeted at-risk students: At Lark, both math and reading scores improved significantly for the intersession group; at Brady, LEP intersession students posted significant gains in reading; and at Palm Avenue, the Chapter 1 students also demonstrated significant gains in reading scores.

Pupil and Teacher Absentee Rates
One of the concerns sometimes expressed about multi-track year-round schools is that because students do not all attend school at the same time, some students may see this as an opportunity to unofficially "go off track" at times when they should be attending school. Although the research suggests this does not usually happen (Quinlan, 1987), we nonetheless felt it was important to test. Table 7 shows the student absence rates at both the experimental and control schools for the period 1988–1989 to 1990–1991.

Both Brady and Palm saw slight to moderate *decreases* in absenteeism of students during this period. Only Lark had an increase in absenteeism, which is unexplained by our data. However, the reader will note that the absenteeism rose to a level only slightly higher than that of the control school for 1990–1991 and prior to that was substantially lower than its control.

Table 7
Average Number of Days Absent per Student
1988–1989 to 1990–1991

School	1988–1989	1989–1990	1990–1991	1989 to 1991 difference
Lark	7.0	8.0	9.3	+2.3
Control for Lark	8.6	9.5	9.0	+0.4
Brady	6.3	6.0	6.2	–0.1
Control for Brady	6.9	5.9	6.0	–0.9
Palm	8.5	6.4	6.4	–2.1
Control for Palm	7.8	6.3	6.2	–1.6

We found little guidance from the literature as to what the effects of the extended year might be on teacher absenteeism. However, we hypothesized that it would probably rise somewhat, in part as a percentage of the increase in days worked, and probably an additional amount resulting from teachers' needs to take care of business that might otherwise have been conducted during traditional vacation time. Table 8 displays the findings on teacher absenteeism for the period 1988–1989 to 1990–1991.

Most notable are the extremely low absentee rates at both Lark and Palm. At these schools, the typical teacher was not absent more than 2 to 3 days during the whole (extended) year. Both of these schools experienced marginal increases in teacher absenteeism. However, at Palm the increase represents only a fraction more than would be expected as a percentage of the increased number of days worked, and at Lark the rate was somewhat artificially inflated in 1990–1991 by pregnancies experienced by 25% of the staff. Nonetheless, teacher absenteeism at both Lark and Palm was considerably lower than at the control schools, even though the teachers were working 20% more days.

Table 8
Average Number of Days Absent per Teacher
1988–1989 to 1990–1991

School	1988–1989	1989–1990	1990–1991	1989 to 1991 difference
Lark	2.0	3.0	3.7	+1.7
Control for Lark	7.8	6.1	5.7	–2.1
Brady	7.8	8.1	7.6	–0.2
Control for Brady	7.8	7.3	—	—
Palm	1.2	1.8	2.0	+0.8
Control for Palm	2.7	3.2	4.0	+1.3

Note: A dash indicates that data are not available or that the category is inapplicable for that particular school.

Brady actually registered a slight drop in absenteeism over the 3-year period though its rate was higher than that of the other two schools. It would seem most accurate to characterize teacher absenteeism at Brady as remaining relatively steady over the 3-year period.

Parent, Teacher, and Student Satisfaction
Parents. Each of the Orchard schools was asked to survey the attitudes of its parents with respect to the experimental program by the end of the first year of implementation. All three schools repeated the survey in the second year and results were very consistent across the 2 years. Each school developed its own instruments, which were distributed anonymously and which included questions that reflected the concerns of the site. All of these surveys were used to collect process data to help each school understand the impact of its program on students and families and to make corrections where indicated. Hence, questions are not parallel across sites. However, each did ask a question about parents' level of satisfaction with the program. Table 9 displays the parents' response to these questions.

Table 9
Parent Satisfaction

School	Year	Number	Percentage responding	% Satisfied/very satisfied
Lark	1990–1991	104	80	70 (non-Hmong 81)
Brady	1990–1991	205	40	85
Palm	1989–1990[a]	264	43	96

[a]1989–1990 data were used because the number of respondents in this year was much larger than for the 1990–1991 survey. Results, however, were very consistent across the 2 years.

Overall, parent satisfaction with the program has been quite high. Substantially more than 60% of the parents expressed satisfaction with the program. The lowest approval was at Lark where 70% of parents expressed overall approval of the program; however, when the responses of the Hmong parents are separated out, the approval rating rises to 81%. Only 39% of the 28 Hmong families returning the survey expressed approval of the program. Similarly, when asked if they would prefer the year-round program or a traditional program, 65% of non-Hmong parent voted for the year-round program; none of the Hmong parents indicated this preference.

A separate, small study of the Hmong parents attitudes was conducted. A representative sampling of 10 Hmong families was interviewed to help us understand the source of their lower approval rating of the program. Most of these families expressed some confusion about the program, and felt that if their children were not in this program they would be able to attend school for more days during the year. Their preference was for a longer school year. This was somewhat ironic since the Hmong children were disproportionately represented in the intersession classes, which effectively lengthened their school year beyond the standard 180 to as many as 220 days. Many of the Hmong parents also expressed some frustration with not being able to communicate effectively with the school and had reservations about whether the school was sensitive to their cultural group. Although there are no Southeast Asian teachers on the staff, two Hmong aides work with students on a daily basis and serve as liaisons with the homes. The school has also made efforts to translate notices into the native language and to survey the Hmong parents in their own tongue.

Brady parents were highly supportive of the program at that school, with an 85% approval rating. They also felt that their children were happy, with 88% agreeing that their children liked school. At Brady, however, the school had previously experimented with a single-track year-round schedule, and the administration was interested in knowing how parents compared this multitrack experience with the previous year-round experience. Fifty-one percent of parents stated that they preferred to remain in the Orchard model; 19% preferred the single track; 24% expressed a preference for a traditional calendar; and 6% had no preference.

Of the 264 families returning the survey at Palm Avenue School, 96% expressed that they were "satisfied" or "very satisfied" with the Orchard program. Only 1% gave it a negative approval rating, indicating that they felt "improvement was needed." Eighty percent of these parents also contended that their children liked the scheduling.

Another way that parents express their satisfaction or dissatisfaction with a program is with their feet. Although we acknowledge that this is less of an option for lower income families, no more than two families at any site requested transfers to other schools when the program was begun.

Two of the schools (Lark and Brady) also asked parents about their opinion of the intersession program. At Lark, 73% of the parents whose children had attended intersession felt that it had helped them (this figure was 58% for the Hmong parents). Seventy percent of the parents of intersession students at Brady contended that their children had benefited from the program.

Among the reasons that parents most commonly cite for liking the program were (a) increased flexibility, (b) the belief that their children retain more of what they learn, and (c) liking the spaced vacations. The most common reasons that parents cited for being unhappy were (a) scheduling conflicts with other siblings who are on traditional school schedules and (b) child-care problems.

Teachers. Teachers were surveyed in all of the schools, using the same instrument, at the end of the first year of implementation, again several months into the 2nd year, and in the spring of 1992—the 3rd year of implementation. The response rate for the first survey was 74% ($n = 42$); most of the missing surveys were from the school with the largest number of teachers (Palm Avenue). The response rate for the second survey was 100% ($n = 63$), and the third survey yielded a response rate of 97% ($n = 64$; see Table 10).

At the end of the first year, 64% of the teachers indicated that they were either satisfied or very satisfied with the program. Only three (7%) stated that they were not satisfied. By the time the second survey was completed during the 2nd year of implementation, only one school had suffered any teacher losses (two at Palm Avenue), and 92% of the teachers claimed to be satisfied with the program. Two teachers (3%) were very unsatisfied. In the 3rd year, 98% of the teachers reported being moderately or very satisfied with the program. One teacher was moderately dissatisfied. These findings are consistent with the literature on teacher satisfaction in year-round schools. While teachers may at first be reluctant to try a year-round schedule, most teachers who have taught in a year-round school prefer it over the traditional calendar (Quinlan, 1987). However, unlike teachers in most year-round schools, these teachers did not have the frequent breaks that are commonly cited as the most attractive aspect of this alternative calendar.

Students. While none of the schools was specifically asked to survey their students' attitudes, all were interested in doing so and collected data during the 2nd year of implementation. Lark school surveyed all of its students in the third grade and above; 99 students returned surveys. Of these, 72% claimed to like the year-round program, and 23% said they wished they could be in school *all year(!).* Forty-seven percent of students said they liked the intersession programs; 32% said they did not; and 21% had no opinion. Most negative comments about the program centered around students' missing their friends while they were off track.

Table 10
Teacher Satisfaction

School and year	Teachers responding		Number responding				
	Number	Percentage	Very satisfied	Satisfied	Neutral[a]	Unsatisfied	Very unsatisfied
Lark							
1989–1990	6	86	5	1	0	0	0
1990–1991	8	100	1	4	2	0	1
1991–1992	6	86	3	2	0	1	0
Brady							
1989–1990	19[b]	86	11	4	2	0	1
1990–1991	19	86	13	6	0	0	0
1991–1992	22	100	20	2	0	0	0
Palm							
1989–1990	17	56	10	3	1	3	0
1990–1991	37	100	29	6	2	0	0
1991–1992	36	97	26	10	0	0	0

[a] The neutral catgory was removed from the 1991–1992 survey to force teachers' responses. "Satisfied" and "Unsatisfied" were consequently changed to "Moderately Satisfied" and "Moderately Unsatisfied."
[b] One teacher responded to survey, but did not answer this question.

Brady surveyed all of its students in Grades 4 to 6. About two thirds of the students responded. Only 42% of these students preferred the year-round schedule, while 58% said they would prefer to be on a schedule that allowed them to all have the same vacation times as their friends. Interestingly, of those students who preferred the year-round schedule, a number commented that one of the chief benefits was the opportunity to get away from some kids for a while. The primary reason students gave for not liking the program was that they missed their friends when they were away from school.

Palm Avenue School did not distribute surveys to its students. Instead, it asked all third to eighth graders to write a paragraph on how they felt about the year-round program. While the school did not attempt to tabulate negative and positive responses, most students responded that they like the program. Students gave many reasons for liking the program, but their chief reason for not liking it was that they missed their friends when they were off track.

DISCUSSION

Overall, the Orchard experiment would appear to be quite successful. The original implementation criteria have all been met, and most of the effectiveness criteria were also met, some at a level considerably higher than one might have hoped for. None of the schools has lost ground academically in any area, and all have posted significantly improved scores in some areas. The achievement scores are particularly encouraging in light of the fact that other studies have suggested that achievement effects may not be seen from such a program for as long as 4 years (Shepard & Baker, 1977). An increase in school capacity and a small reduction in class size have also been achieved while maintaining high levels of satisfaction on the part of parents and teachers.

Waiting lists were so long to get into Palm Avenue School that the district converted two more schools to the Orchard model in 1990–1991 and immediately filled them with both teachers and students eager to participate. Currently, several other schools are converting, at least partially, to the Orchard program, and the district has placed all schools on a 60–15 calendar to facilitate future conversions. Brady school is a model school for its district and, in addition to having a long waiting list of teachers who wish to teach there, plays host to numerous visitors coming to investigate its possibilities.

Nonetheless, we have learned a great deal from the experiment and re-thought a number of aspects of the program. Intersession programs appear to be spectacular successes where the schools are able to implement them fully. However there are a number of impediments to successful implementation. The channeling of moneys to these programs was more complicated than we had initially expected. Principals do not always have full authority over their budgets, and there are many competing interests in the schools. Perhaps the biggest program is that of equity. While the intersession programs were targeted for at-risk children, many of these children did not return to school for the program. To some extent this can be remedied by providing better transportation and after-program child care. However, unless students are compelled to attend school for extra days, some of the students most in need of extra help will probably always evade it. Acknowledging this fact, some teachers were reluctant to give up the pull-out instruction for their at-risk students. And, of course, to the extent that a school continued to support pull-out instruction, it diluted the necessary support to mount an effective intersession program.

Other problems that arose with the intersession programming were the following:

1. *Coordination.* It takes a fair amount of time to plan and organize the intersession program; this may be most possible in larger schools where there are more resources to draw on.

2. *The states' requirement that a certificated teacher be in charge of every class.* This eliminated the possibility of using excellent resources in the community unless a certificated teacher would also be present in the classes.

3. *Hiring of high quality staff.* Intersession teachers were not hired as full-time teachers; hence, the most qualified teachers were always at risk for being hired away to another full-time position (that paid better and offered benefits).

4. *Space limitations.* These were all over-crowded schools where space is at a premium. The schools were amazingly inno-

vative, using libraries, cafeterias, portables, and off-site facilities, but it was always a struggle to find sufficient space that was accessible to students.

Some of the intersession coursework can, and should, be offered by resource specialists in the schools. This is especially true in cases where students would otherwise have been pulled out of class to spend time with these people. However, intersession programs were also envisioned as opportunities to expose students to things that were not offered in the regular curriculum, as an opportunity to explore different topics through different, and possibly more interactive methods. The intersessions were supposed to teach skills in the context of a qualitatively different education experience. Some of this happened, but not quite as much as we had hoped. It should be noted, however, that schools continue to solicit resources from their communities and new partnerships are evolving as a result of these ongoing efforts. In fact, this has provided an important catalyst for increased community involvement in at least two of the schools.

> **Intersession programs were also envisioned as opportunities to expose students to things that were not offered in the regular curriculum.**

Personnel is another area in which some unresolved issues exist. The kinds of teachers who opt into an experiment such as this tend to be high-energy people, and often without young children of their own. Also, more experienced teachers tended to be among the most enthusiastic about the program, no doubt in part because their compensation also tended to be at the top of the scale. But one suspects that many of the teachers who opted into the program or who were very enthusiastic were also very successful teachers who had made teaching a lifetime career because of their unusual ability as teachers. Nonetheless, it is clear that extended work contracts are clearly not for everyone, and it is difficult to know for what percentage of the teachers they would be a reasonable option. Both Brady and Palm have long waiting lists of teachers who want the opportunity to work an extended contract; on the other hand, teachers have not been clamoring for these positions at Lark.

After 2 years in the program, approximately one fourth of the teachers surveyed said they would like to return to a shorter contract in the future. By the 3rd year, with only one teacher having left the program, three teachers (6%) said they preferred to return to a 9-month contract. We believe that teachers should be given the option of working different length contracts, and an 11-month school year may offer more possibilities toward that end than a 9-month school. In any case, we have come to think that teachers should have a choice from year to year to negotiate this.

> Both teachers and students commented that off-track breaks occasionally brought welcome relief.

The greatest threat of "burnout," however, may be for the principal. Principals in 9-month schools already work nearly year round; adding the extra months to the school calendar, and the extra students to the campus, can put an enormous burden on the principal. The principals in this study, like their teachers, were high-energy "doers." They commented that if they weren't running the school, they weren't likely to be lying on a beach anyway; as a group they rarely complained about the workload, but it was evident that being a principal of an extended calendar school was "a special calling." It should be noted, however, that they uniformly contended that it was easier to manage an Orchard plan school than other year-round schools because all their teachers were present throughout the year and hence they did not have to deal with scheduling classrooms, teachers, and faculty meetings on a revolving basis.

While parents and teachers were quite supportive of the program and the majority of both preferred it over other options, students were clearly ambivalent—and almost always for the same reason: They miss their friends when they are off track. Interestingly, however, this played out in several ways. Teachers consistently commented that students were so anxious to return to school (to see their friends) after breaks, that every 3 weeks began with a new burst of enthusiasm in the classroom. Students were more openly conscious of wanting to be in school. It was also interesting to note that both teachers and students commented that off-track breaks occasionally brought welcome relief from personalities with whom they did not get along well. Schools reported fewer "incidents" on the playground, a reduction in the number of office referrals, and a healthier climate in the classroom with the changing classroom dynamic. Teachers also consistently observed that students appear to have more opportunities to take on new roles in the classroom; as the "stars" tracked out, other students (perhaps those who suffered under the shadow of the acknowledged class star) would take their place.

Teaming has broken down the traditional isolation of many of the teachers.

This raises the issue of what it is like for a teacher to teach in a classroom whose student composition is constantly changing. This feature of the experiment was the single greatest impediment to enticing schools to apply to participate in the experiment. The Orchard teachers mention how other teachers in their district refer to them as crazy and many even refuse to observe at the school because they consider the idea so outlandish. Because of this strong reaction on the part of many teachers, we had hypothesized that this could end up being the Achilles heel of the program.

We were literally stunned after the first teacher surveys came back and the first teacher meetings were held; we were told over and again that the single best feature of the program was the rotation of students. Teachers felt that at first it was more work to develop new routines for working with students, but they felt very good about the fact that they *had* to know where every student was in the curriculum all the time. Communication with homes was increased as teachers sent off work packets and student reports with exiting students; students were working more in groups and taking more responsibility for their own learning; and the social environment of the classroom was enhanced by the breaking down of cliques and the increased participation of students. One also suspects that the teaming that resulted from restructuring the curricula plays a role in teacher attitudes; many teachers contend that they could not do this without a team approach. And this teaming has broken down the traditional isolation of many of the teachers.

CONCLUSIONS

1. Year-round or extended year programs are feasible for many communities, and with increased exposure and some degree of input into planning such programs, parents and teachers are likely to find them to be satisfactory alternatives to traditional school calendars.

2. Year-round calendars can open the door to many kinds of innovation in curriculum, instructional delivery, student grouping, and teacher contracts, if communities wish to take advantage of those opportunities.

3. Intersession programs can be an important adjunct to the regular school curriculum and may provide support and enrichment for children who need an additional academic boost. However, mounting them successfully probably requires considerable support from a variety of sources.

4. Extended year and year-round programs can work to reduce class size, at least marginally, without additional cost. However, the degree to which this size reduction will affect teacher satisfaction remains a researchable question.

5. Teachers can (and probably should) be given the option to contract for different work schedules. Some teachers want to work a longer year for greater remuneration, and schools and districts can benefit both financially and educationally from these teachers' choices.

6. Schools may find that experimentation with a changing classroom dynamic, by whatever means this is achieved, can promote more positive attitudes in the classroom and expand the number of positive roles available to students.

If the overarching purpose of restructuring is to increase student learning and if this is best accomplished in a collaborative, self-renewing learning environment, this study suggests that the unique features of the Orchard Plan experiment support and facilitate that purpose.

NOTES

1. Neither the literature nor common parlance systematically distinguishes between schools that truly operate year round without any break and those with extended year calendars. Many different scheduling options are available to schools, and each varies in the way it schedules instruc-

tional blocks and break or vacation times for students and/or teachers. In this paper we use *year-round* school synonymously with *extended year.*

2. Extended year contracts were negotiated independently with the local bargaining unit for the teachers at each site; hence, the contracts differed in detail. However, teacher benefits such as sick leave and retirement pay were generally augmented to reflect the 20% longer working year.

3. Demographic descriptions of the schools presented here differ somewhat from the data displayed in Table 2 because of rapid demographic shifts in the school, especially at Lark. These descriptions are based on the 1991–1992 school year; Table 2 reflects 1988–1989 data.

4. One teacher was "bumped" due to lower seniority after the reshuffling of teaching staff resulting from the former principal's illness: however, this teacher had expressed a desire to remain at the school.

5. *Single track year round* generally refers to a year-round or extended year schedule in which the summer break is shortened in favor of including several breaks during the year. Everyone, all students and teachers, cycle in and out of school at the same time. This type of schedule is sometimes implemented for educational reasons, but it does not increase the capacity of the school.

REFERENCES

Alliance for Achievement. (1989). *Building the value-based school community.* Chicago: Academic Development Institute.

Brown, P., & Haycock, K. (1984). *Excellence for whom?* Oakland, CA: The Achievement Council.

Cagampang, H., Garms, W., Greenspan, T., & Guthrie, J. (1985). *Teacher supply and demand in California: Is the reserve pool a realistic source of supply?* Unpublished manuscript. Berkeley: University of California, Policy Analysis for California Education.

California Department of Education. (1991). *Language census.* Sacramento, CA: Office of Bilingual Education.

California Department of Education. (1992). *Fact sheet, 1992–93.* Sacramento, CA: Author.

Cohen, E. (1972). *Designing groupwork.* New York: Teachers College Press.

Cuban, L. (1992, March 11). Please. No more facts, just better teaching. *Education Week, 11,* 40.

Darling-Hammond, L. (1984). *Beyond the commission reports: The coming crisis in teaching.* Santa Monica, CA: RAND. (R-3177-RC).

Gartner, A., & Lipsky, D. (1987). Beyond special education: Toward a quality system for all students. *Harvard Educational Review, 57,* 367–395.

Gordon, D. (1991, February). *Preparing California youth for the next century: Demographic change and student access to work and citizenship.* Presentation to the Sociology of Education Conference, Asilomar, February 15.

Handleman, J., & Harris, S. (1984). Can summer vacation be detrimental to learning? An empirical look. *Exceptional Children, 31,* 151–157.

Kimbrough, J., & Hill, P. (1981). *Problems of implementing multiple categorical education programs.* Santa Monica, CA: RAND. (R-2957-ED).

Lyman, L., & Foyle, H. (1990). *Cooperative grouping for administrators.* Washington, DC: National Education Association.

McDonnell, L., & Pascal, A. (1988). *Teacher unions and educational reform.* Santa Monica, CA: RAND. (JRE-02).

McLaughlin, M. (1987). Lessons from past implementation research. *Educational Evaluation and Policy Analysis, 9,* 171–178.

Murnane, R., Singer, J., Willett, J., Kemple, J. & Olsen, R. (1991). *Who will teach?* Cambridge, MA: Harvard University Press.

New York State Department of Education and State University of New York. (1978). *Learning, retention, and forgetting* (Tech. Rep. No. 5. A Report to the Board of Regents of the State of New York). Albany, NY: Author.

Oakes, J. (1985). *Keeping track.* New Haven, CT: Yale University Press. Policy Analysis for California Education. (1991). *Conditions of education in California 1990.* Berkeley: University of California.

Quinlan, C. (1987). *Year round education: Year round opportunities. A study of year round education in California.* Sacramento: California State Department of Education (ERIC Document Reproduction Service No. ED 2285 272).

Shepard, M., & Baker, K. (1977). *Year round schools.* Lexington, MA: Lexington Books.

Slavin, R., (1990). *Cooperative learning: Theory, research, and practice.* Englewood Cliffs, NJ: Prentice-Hall.

Snyder, T., & Hoffman, C. (1991). *Digest of education statistics.* Washington, DC: U.S. Department of Education, Office of Educational Research and Improvement (National Center for Education Statistics). (NCES 91-660).

Stedman, J., & Jordan, K. F. (1986). *Education reform reports: Content and impact.* Washington, DC: Congressional Research Service. (Report No. 86-56 EPW).

Seven Rules to Year-Round Schooling: Research and Dialogue Make Implementation Possible

by Gary A. Knox

Readers of the daily newspaper weather pages know three things about Yuma, Ariz. Yuma standards last in the alphabetical listing of National Weather Service reporting stations. Yuma typically appears in the reddest portion of the national weather map. Yuma is often the nation's hot spot.

Our local newspaper headline on June 27, 1990 read: "Heat Wave Continues to Hammer Yuma." What the headline did not say was: "Wow! 122 degrees!"

As superintendent of an elementary school system in Yuma, I sat on a hot seat for other important reasons. I had to find ways to avoid overcrowded schools and improve student achievement. Moreover, I had to find solutions—hot weather or not—in a climate of sharply declining revenues.

Two short summers after our record-setting heat, a mid-summer newspaper headline stated: "Many In Crane Start School Soon." In headline parlance, "soon" meant the following day.

HALF-BAKED NOTIONS?

We had found a solution. In short, more than 5,000 students now attend our six schools on a single-track year-round calendar. Year-round means the traditional summer vacation is broken into parts and redistributed in segments throughout the

From *The School Administrator,* vol. 51, no. 3, March 1994, pp. 22–24.
© 1994 by the American Association of School Administrators. Reprinted with permission.

year. A 45-15 schedule allows our students to attend school in four 45-day periods separated by 15-day intersessions (vacations).

Some believed we'd been out in the midday sun too long when we announced we planned to investigate a year-round calendar. Imagine year-round education in a community where the thermometer shatters 110 degrees for weeks on end, breaking the century mark at least four months annually. Some thought us half-baked to even consider this calendar change, but nevertheless we started school in mid-summer on a single-track modified 45-15 calendar.

> Year-round education can be implemented anywhere—when the community is ready.

Executive Director Charles Ballinger of the National Association for Year-Round Education cites our experience as an example of success under improbable circumstances. He has noted that if Yuma can have year-round schools in the hot, low desert climate of southern Arizona, one can implement year-round schooling anywhere.

ESSENTIAL STEPS

Year-round education can be implemented anywhere—when the community is ready. That's what this story is about. Is the community—in our case, a farming community producing most of the nation's winter lettuce, cauliflower, and broccoli— ready to abandon the nine-month agrarian school calendar? Will a community break from tradition to gain better student achievement, a reduced tax burden, and/or less crowded schools?

Our decision to make this radical move was considered carefully over three or four years. The decision emerged after extensive research and considerable community dialogue. As we reviewed, cussed, discussed, and shaped a workable year-round education plan, I came to realize some essential rules to bring effective implementation in an unsure community.

Implementation Rule No. 1: Do your homework before seriously initiating the idea of year-round education with your community. Before you talk about year-round education, know what this concept means. Know how a year-round education structure can work. Know the difference between single-track and multi-track. Understand 45-15, the Orchard Plan, Concept Six, and other typical year-round education calendars. Know major drawbacks. Know the difference between real problems and false perceptions.

Our dialogue with parents and staff started with literally dozens of general questions, such as:

- How can we keep energy costs to a minimum during the hot summer months?

- How is a concentrated physical cleaning of a school to be done?

- How are classrooms shared?

- How will classes be organized?

- What assurance do we have about siblings being on the same track?

- What happens to interscholastic athletic programs?

Be prepared to respond to a broad array of questions. We had reasonable replies, but we assigned a community task force the responsibility to investigate and give answers.

A PUBLIC PROCESS
Implementation Rule No. 2: Involve your community in making recommendations about a possible year-round conversion.
To involve our community we met with residents. We talked to parents. We held public forums. We met in schools. We spoke in homes. We sent information home with students. We talked to staff. We brought the governing board along, step by step. We published our findings for all to read and review. We answered question after question. We researched year-round education until we knew more than the experts. (Then we picked expert brains to be confident we hadn't missed anything.)

We formed investigation teams of parents, citizens, business representatives, and staff members. Participants were selected for their open minds, not for their positions on year-round education. We did the things the textbooks suggest.

We used an NAYRE publication, *Year-Round Education Resource Guidebook*, which provides some basic guidelines for moving toward a decision. We adapted those guidelines to our circumstances. In all, five community-based teams helped at various stages in the decision-making process. These teams recommended whether, when, and how to move to year-round education.

Implementation Rule No. 3: Form a support group to solidify acceptance about the recommendations, since every proposed action has detractors.

> Principals and directors, certified and classified, understood that year-round education meant better schools.

As we approached a board decision, four of the five board members told me they supported the year-round education recommendation. While unanimity is preferred, one board member had declared opposition at the outset. Everyone understood well in advance there would be one negative vote.

Then I blundered. I failed to follow Implementation Rule No. 3. Even after a small, vocal, well-organized opposition emerged, I believed the recommendation was secure. Indeed, I actually discouraged formation of a pro-recommendation group. I thought the decision for year-round schooling was firm. After all, board members had told me they supported the recommendation.

My failure to form a support group resulted in much heartache. Voices in opposition forced additional public meetings. We had to poll for parental preferences. Letters to the editor became heated. Board support wavered. Hope for a clear board vote in support of the recommendation appeared dead. While governing board views about the value of year-round education had not changed, the political landscape had!

RALLYING COLLEAGUES
Implementation Rule No. 4: Should your path become rocky, encourage those you trust and respect to tell you like it is.
I told my management team that I was discouraged by eroding board support. I considered throwing in the towel. Collectively they said "no!" Principals and directors, certified and classified, understood that year-round education meant better schools. Year-round education would bring better facilities, more learning by our children, and substantial tax reductions or tax avoidance over the years.

This unanimous management team support led to a new plan. We knew families in our district were split between embracing year-round education and continuing the traditional pattern. Our solution, therefore, allowed every family to choose between a 45-15 year-round calendar and a nine-month calendar. This dual-track format was immediately supported by the board and the community. Opposition vanished.

Required to administer two tracks in every school, all principals accomplished the task willingly and enthusiastically. Despite the dual-track complication, our single-track 45-15 experience proved to be better than anyone could have hoped. Only then did year-round education cease to be some theoretical way to educate our students better.

Staff, parents, and students rallied to support the program. Most became convinced it was best for student learning. And those skeptics who were concerned about year-round schools in our hot summers? They too rallied to support the program.

Implementation Rule No. 5: Develop a multi-year plan for moving toward and fully implementing year-round education.
While "field testing" our two-track experiment, we wrote a five-year plan. If year-round education worked successfully, how would we expand it?

The plan considered our new-found commitment to the year-round format, our anticipated student growth, and our projected annual bonding capacity. Members of the management team made a public presentation of the plan to the governing board. I stayed on the sidelines. The presentation clearly demonstrated to the community that year-round schooling was supported by all principals and administrators.

STATISTICAL STUDIES
Implementation Rule No. 6: Collect data on the issues that are raised within the community as you initiate year-round education, regardless of the size of your first program.
We addressed three major issues. These included the impact of the hot summer months, skepticism about whether a 45-15 schedule would improve learning environments, and questions about perceived prohibitive year-round schooling costs.

We surveyed. We reviewed records. We found that 45-15 students had no problem with the heat; they'd played in it all their lives. Teachers found students needed virtually no review time after intersessions; students appeared to be returning from long weekends.

Authentic assessment data seemed to support broader achievement findings. Electrical costs were within the range previously predicted by our community researchers. (Our schools already were air-conditioned. Utility costs increased about 10 percent.) Added salary costs proved minimal as we employed a strategy of reordering work-year patterns to coincide with the new school attendance arrangement.

> Authentic assessment data seemed to support broader achievement findings.

By collecting data on these issues, we verified the findings and predictions of those who had initially recommended year-round education. They were right. Year-round schooling can be implemented in the summer heat. It does appear to improve student learning and can be cost effective.

Implementation Rule No. 7: Remain flexible, keeping focused on your real goals.

Year-round education was never our goal. Our two goals were to improve student achievement and delay, if not escape, overcrowded schools. Year-round education was selected as a means to those ends.

As opposition and obstacles arose, we easily worked around them since we weren't committed to installing a specific year-round education model. We didn't stray from our real goals. Year-round structure, timelines, participation, etc., shifted without loss of direction because we accommodated emerging concerns.

For instance, at one time or another we variously planned for a 60-20 calendar, separate year-round and nine-month schools, installing the Oxnard curriculum model, and a host of other proposed actions that never experienced the heat of a Yuma day. We remained wedded to finding a way to reach our goals.

CONVINCING EVIDENCE

Year-round education was not a solution in search of a problem. We pursued year-round education vigorously only after investigations led us to believe student achievement would increase. We found evidence year-round students perform as well as, but usually better than, students on the typical school calendar.

> Our investigators were convinced year-round education could increase classroom space despite restricted school budgets.

The primary source for this conclusion was the Oxnard, Calif., Elementary School District's longitudinal study in 1991. This study clearly demonstrates advantages for year-round education students. We were impressed since Oxnard's demographics parallel ours. Each district serves a large student population of Mexican ancestry. A 1993 review of 13 studies by Leslie Six, a Southern California consultant hired by NAYRE, confirmed the Oxnard academic achievement findings.

Second, our investigators were convinced year-round education could increase classroom space despite restricted school budgets. A host of studies conducted in a variety of settings supported this conclusion, notably those in Jefferson County, Colo. (conducted internally in 1990) and Cherry Creek, Colo. (conducted by Price Waterhouse in 1991), as well as several in California districts (Visalia, 1988; Oxnard, 1991; San Diego City Schools, 1989). Our own experiences in two years lend support to these cost saving/cost avoiding studies.

We also understand the need for a policy spelling out the conditions that determine when a single-track school converts to multi-track. Our experience, confirmed by data from many districts, shows when a school exceeds its capacity by about 15 percent, it becomes cost effective to change to multi-track.

Within a year or two we expect to convert our junior high school from a single-track calendar to a multi-track calendar. With more than 1,150 students, the school is overcrowded. A magnet elementary school also will convert to multi-track because it exceeds its capacity by 15 percent.

RADICAL CHANGE

Successful conversion to year-round education has helped the Crane Elementary School District attack two problems. The radical calendar change has led to better student learning and it gave us a means to handle significant student growth without increasing bonded indebtedness.

As you weigh a year-round format, consider the seven rules for implementation. You'll have a stronger program and save yourself and your board members unnecessary heat (regardless of your local weather) when you are well prepared.

Authors

Julia Anderson, a former special assistant to the National Council on Vocational Education, is a consultant to the Department of Education. She is helping to organize the Interagency Technology Office, which will direct the Technology Learning Challenge Grants.

Robert D. Becker is dean of arts and sciences at Clayton State College in Morrow, Georgia.

James C. Bradford Jr. is the superintendent of Buena Vista City Public Schools in Buena Vista, Virginia. He is a national consultant and speaker on topics related to the year-round school movement in the United States.

Wallace D. Campbell, after thirty-two years in public education, currently works with mentally retarded adults for the Greene County Board of MR/DD in Xenia, Ohio. He is the author of many professional and news articles.

Robin Cash is director of Institutional Studies at Western State College of Colorado. She was the project director of Western Scholars Year and chaired the steering committee that planned and implemented Western's year-round calendar.

Larry L. Dlugosh is associate professor and department chair in the Department of Educational Administration at the University of Nebraska-Lincoln. He is the coauthor of *The School Superintendency: New Responsibilities, New Leadership.*

Paul Edwards, associate professor of communication and theatre at Western State College of Colorado, directs its honors program. He served on the Western Scholars Year Steering Committee and helped implement course time blocks in the Scholars Year schedule.

Judy Fish is assistant superintendent for educational services at Palmdale School District and an instructor at Chapman University. She serves on the California Year Round State Advisory Committee.

Patricia Gándara is associate professor of education at the University of California, Davis, and president of the Sociology of Education Association. She is author of *Over the Ivy Walls: The Educational Mobility of Low Income Chicanos.*

Don Glines is the director of the Educational Futures Project in Sacramento, California. He has authored fourteen books and has delivered nearly one thousand addresses on educational futures, alternatives, and continuous learning.

Teresa Arámbula Greenfield is associate professor of education and women's studies at the University of Hawaii at Manoa in Honolulu, Hawaii. Her major areas of research focus on the interrelationships between science education and gender.

Morton Inger specializes in policy research in education, sociology, and politics. He is associated with the Institute on Education and the Economy at Teachers College, Columbia University, and is the author of *Politics and Reality in an American City.*

Gary A. Knox has been superintendent of the Crane Elementary School District in Yuma, Arizona, since 1987.

Sue E. Mutchler is a senior policy associate at Southwest Educational Development Laboratory in Austin, Texas. She is the author of articles on state education policy issues, including governance and education/health/human services coordination.

Paul S. Piper is an information specialist/writer/researcher for the Center of Excellence in Disaster Management and Humanitarian Assistance. He has produced nonfiction, fiction, and poetry for more than fifty publications.

Kim VanderHooven is an academic adviser at Heidelberg College in Maumee, Ohio. She received a master's degree in counseling from Bowling Green State University.

Frank Venturo is associate vice president of academic affairs and a professor of communication at Western State College of Colorado. He developed the Western Scholars Year concept and composed its original proposal.

Acknowledgments

Grateful acknowledgment is made to the following authors and agents for their permission to reprint copyrighted materials.

SECTION 1
The American Association of School Administrators (AASA) for "Alternative Approaches to Organizing the School Day and Year: A National Commission Examines New Structures for Improving Student Learning" by Julia Anderson. From *The School Administrator,* vol. 51, no. 3, pp. 8–11, 15, March 1994. Copyright © 1994 by AASA. Reprinted with permission. All rights reserved.

Don Glines for "YRE Basics: History, Methods, Concerns, Future" by Don Glines. Paper presented at the annual meeting of the National Association for Year-Round Education (San Diego, California, February 12–16, 1994). Copyright © 1994 by Don Glines. Reprinted with permission. All rights reserved.

Don Glines for "YRE Rationale: Philosophy and Methods" by Don Glines. Paper presented at the annual meeting of the National Association for Year-Round Education (Orlando, Florida, February 17–22, 1996). Copyright © 1996 by Don Glines. Reprinted with permission. All rights reserved.

James C. Bradford Jr. for "Year-Round Education: Impact on Support Services, Transportation, Operation, Facilities, and Maintenance" by James C. Bradford Jr. Paper presented at the annual meeting of the Association of School Business Officials of Maryland and Washington, D.C. (Arnold, Maryland, January 1995). Copyright © 1995 by James C. Bradford Jr. Reprinted with permission. All rights reserved.

Southwest Educational Development Laboratory (SEDL) for "Year-Round Education" by Sue E. Mutchler. From *SEDL Insights,* no. 2, pp. 1–3, 5–6, March 1993. Copyright © 1993 by SEDL. Reprinted with permission. All rights reserved.

SECTION 2
Pacific Region Educational Laboratory (PREL) for "Year-Round Schools: The Star of the Sea Model" by Paul S. Piper. From *Educational Innovations in the Pacific,* vol. 1, no. 1, pp. 1–4, May 1994. Copyright © 1994 by PREL. Reprinted with permission. All rights reserved.

James C. Bradford Jr. for "Making Year-Round Education (YRE) Work in Your District: A Nationally Recognized Single Track High School Model" by James C. Bradford Jr. Paper presented at the annual meeting of the National School Boards Association (Anaheim, California, March 22–31, 1993). Copyright © 1993 by James C. Bradford Jr. Reprinted with permission. All rights reserved.

Educational Research Service (ERS) for "Year-Round Schooling for Academically At-Risk Students: Outcomes and Perceptions of Participants in an Elementary Program" by Wallace D. Campbell. From *ERS Spectrum,* vol. 12, no. 3, pp. 20–24, summer 1994. Copyright © 1994 by ERS. Reprinted with permission. All rights reserved.

ERIC Clearinghouse on Urban Education (ERIC/CUE) for "Year-Round Education: A Strategy for Overcrowded Schools" by Morton Inger. From *ERIC/CUE Digest,* no. 103, pp. 3–4, December 1994. Copyright © 1994 by ERIC/CUE. Reprinted with permission. All rights reserved.

Robin Cash for "Reinventing Community by Changing the Academic Calendar: Changing Time and the Consequences" by Robin Cash, Robert D. Becker, Frank Venturo, and Paul Edwards. Paper presented at the National Conference on Education of the American Association for Higher Education (Washington, D. C., March 14–17, 1993). Copyright © 1993 by Robin G. Cash. Reprinted with permission. All rights reserved.

SECTION 3
Larry L. Dlugosh for "Quality Schools and the Myth of the Nine-Month School Year" by Larry L. Dlugosh. Paper presented at the annual University of Oklahoma National Conference on Creating the Quality School (Oklahoma City, Oklahoma, March 31–April 2, 1994). Copyright © 1994 by Larry L. Dlugosh. Reprinted with permission. All rights reserved.

Kappa Delta Pi, an International Honor Society in Education, for "Year-Round Education: A Case for Change" by Teresa Arámbula

Greenfield. From *The Educational Forum,* vol. 58, no. 3, pp. 252–62, spring 1994. Copyright © 1994 by Kappa Delta Pi, an International Honor Society in Education. Reprinted with permission. All rights reserved.

Kim VanderHooven for "Opinions Regarding Year-Round Education: A Survey Among the Public" by Kim VanderHooven. Unpublished paper from ERIC, 1994, ED 376 603. Copyright © 1994 by Kim VanderHooven. Reprinted with permission. All rights reserved.

American Educational Research Association (AERA) for "Year-Round Schooling as an Avenue to Major Structural Reform" by Patricia Gándara and Judy Fish. From *Educational Evaluation and Policy Analysis,* vol. 16, no. 1, pp. 67–85, spring 1994. Copyright © 1994 by AERA. Reprinted with permission. All rights reserved.

The American Association of School Administrators (AASA) for "Seven Rules to Year-Round Schooling: Research and Dialogue Make Implementation Possible" by Gary A. Knox. From *The School Administrator,* vol. 51, no. 3, pp. 22–24, March 1994. Copyright © 1994 by AASA. Reprinted with permission. All rights reserved.

Index

Training and Publishing Inc.

We Prepare Your Teachers Today
for the Classrooms of Tomorrow

Learn from Our Books and from Our Authors!

Ignite Learning in Your School or District.

SkyLight's team of classroom-experienced consultants can help you foster systemic change for increased student achievement.

Professional development is a process, not an event. SkyLight's seasoned practitioners drive the creation of our on-site professional development programs, graduate courses, research-based publications, interactive video courses, teacher-friendly training materials, and online resources—call SkyLight Training and Publishing Inc. today.

SkyLight specializes in three professional development areas.

Specialty #

Best Practices

We **model** the best practices that result in improved student performance and guided applications.

Specialty #

Making the Innovations Last

We help set up **support** systems that make innovations part of everyday practice in the long-term systemic improvement of your school or district.

Specialty #

How to Assess the Results

We prepare your school leaders to encourage and **assess** teacher growth, **measure** student achievement, and **evaluate** program success.

Contact the SkyLight team and begin a process toward long-term results.

Training and Publishing Inc.

2626 S. Clearbrook Dr., Arlington Heights, IL 60005
800-348-4474 • 847-290-6600 • FAX 847-290-6609

There are

one-story intellects,

two-story intellects, and three-story

intellects with skylights. All fact collectors, who

have no aim beyond their facts, are one-story men. Two-story men

compare, reason, generalize, using the labors of the fact collectors as

well as their own. Three-story men idealize, imagine,

predict—their best illumination comes from

above, through the skylight.

—*Oliver Wendell*

Holmes

Training and Publishing Inc.